What Readers Are Saying About
Dance With The Stars

"Beautifully and clearly presented with an original voice. The material surely has been channeled!"

— LISA RAPHAEL, ST. PETERSBURG, FL

"Every time I come back to this book, my understanding is deepened and a new richness is added to my life."

— DR. KAREN CHAMBERLAIN, TAMPA, FL

"This book is pure Truth for all who are brave enough to see it. God has chosen Kristine as a messenger—my advice is To Listen & Learn now, while you still have the choice. May God Bless and keep you all."

— REV. SHARON LEE BELVIN, CLEARWATER, FL

"An uncommon work for the common man."

— ANONYMOUS

"Your book continues to be a great blessing in my life. I feel the power is not in the words written as much as in the vibration with which they resonate. I believe that it touches that basic vibration within each of us, the universal vibration of Love."

— LINDA COLEMAN, ST. PETERSBURG, FL

"This book is like a bouquet of wild flowers—each page a pure simple gift bathed in the fragrance of love."

— JEAN McGUIRE, DUNEDIN, FL

DANCE
WITH THE
STARS

A Personal Journey to Spirituality

KRISTINE GAY JOHNSON

SPIRITUAL
AWARENESS
PRODUCTIONS
• • •
TARPON SPRINGS, FLORIDA

Library of Congress Catalog Card Number 98-090457
ISBN# 0-9663659-7-6

Printing coordination by Barbara Hagen, Publishers Service Alliance
Cover and interior by Troy Scott Parker, Cimarron Design

Printed in the United States of America by Data Reproductions

Published by
Spiritual Awareness Productions
PO Box 519
Tarpon Springs, Florida 34688-0519
fax 727-943-8184
www.SpiritAware.com

Contents

Acknowledgments

TO MY HUSBAND, LEE, *thank you* for allowing me my differences, for your insight, and for the challenges that continue to hone my Being. I love you.

My dear friend, Jean McGuire, was the first to set eyes on the tender first rough draft of this book. She waded through the sentence fragments and misspellings with her keen Virgo mind, giving encouragement and corrections. Coming full circle, she viewed the work on its last stop before typesetting. Her caring nature and deep friendship is a continuing blessing.

After I met Karen Chamberlain at the Florida Suncoast Writers' Conference in February, 1997, she became central in the editing process. Since the book had not been written from front to back, her new eyes helped regroup and flesh out the information. Even as she helped shape this material, the words she read answered personal questions for which she had been seeking answers. Our heart-connection has been an inspiration for me.

In my home state of Washington, a life-long friend, Glenn Buttkus, added his words of encouragement. Being a powerful wordsmith in his own right, Glenn's enthusiasm for this book sparked my energies, even when the going seemed slow. Our shared interest in metaphysics and this Time of Awakening lent courage to the process.

Rev. Sharon Lee (Suzie) Belvin has been a blessed catalyst in my life. It was from her lips that we both learned of this book, 1½ years before its first word hit paper. She has been a Divine touchstone for me. Through her words and wonderful resonant voice, I have felt and absorbed the vibrations of God's Love. Her accurate information serves to amplify the subtle messages coming into me from Spirit. The depth of my gratitude for having her in my life cannot be put into words.

On a recommendation from Barbara Hagen, I contacted Troy Scott Parker of Cimarron Design in Boulder, Colorado about doing the cover design for this book. His preference to work with spiritual material, the natural beauty of his creations, and the warm smiles from my guides synched the deal. His sensitively artistic eye designed both cover and text. I thank God for putting us together that these words might be brought into the world in such a gentle and beautiful form.

Preface

As I grew up in Washington state, I experienced myself as an outsider. I saw others shaping their lives, using rules I did not understand nor trust. Somehow my life always seemed out-of-synch. I just didn't get it.

In my eighteenth year, I sat in Professor Bill Hoffman's Philosophy class at Highline College, just South of Seattle. He posed a not-too-interesting question to the class. With only peripheral interest, I raised my hand and parroted back the gist of the information from our text. To my undying gratitude, he then asked me a question I will hear until the day I die: "Why is this *your* answer?"

It was as if I had been asleep for a thousand years, and someone had just violently shaken me awake. My silent, large-eyed response took no longer than five seconds before the class moved on to other things. I was left swirling in my mind, as the domino effect started by his question realigned my consciousness.

It had *never occurred to me* that there might be validity in my own perspective. On that day, my amazed mind swung around from its outward observation to a newly found appreciation of myself. A brand new world of possibilities lay open before me.

Throughout my life I have never been much of a joiner of organizations, nor have I had a passion for competition with others. My way has been quiet and contemplative. Certainly as I sat in Professor Hoffman's class in 1965, I had no idea of the adventure that awaited me.

During a consultation with a dear friend and psychic in October 1994, information came out about a book I was going to write. It would provide information to help many people find answers to questions that had been haunting them. It was going to touch many Souls.

I had always enjoyed writing. I had also always harbored a dream of finding a way to help Humanity find peace and answers. But when I heard this information I was dumb struck. Only after the next two years had unfolded was I finally able to recognize the thread that had run through my entire life...

When about fifteen years old, I sat in our family living room resting after our fireworks fun on the 4th of July. From somewhere I had picked up a piece of blank paper in one hand, and still grasped a smoldering punk in the other. With no intention and relaxed mind, I began to touch the punk to the paper, watching peacefully as an image emerged. The "Star Child" figure (shown at the beginning of each chapter in this book) is what appeared in my hands that night. Although the significance of his appearance was unknown to me, I have treasured his company over the years.

Feeling a need to define my position in my college years, I considered myself an agnostic. Although I could not see God, the beauty and majesty I saw everywhere in Nature in Washington state gave rise to a reverence I could not deny.

As I matured, I found authors that spoke to me personally, their words resonating with what I was discovering to be my personal truth. Some of these authors were T. Lobsang Rampa, Yogananda, Richard Bach, Stuart Wilde, Jack Schwarz, Jerry Stocking, and channeled works from Seth (Jane Roberts), Michael Books (Chelsea Quinn Yarbro, Joya Pope, Carol Heideman), and Kryon (Lee Carroll).

Through the years my path crossed those of astrologers and psychics who allowed my imagination to glimpse the deeper currents in my life. Silent observation of my life events and those people surrounding me lent nourishment to my deepening quest: "Why are we here?" "Is there a God?" "What is this whole thing of life all about?"

In the spring of 1994, I awoke from a vivid dream. As the details quickly fled from my memory, I was left with a root impression that stood out with great clarity: in the dream my sense of Joy began to expand. As my Being filled with an awesome flood of joy, I could no longer remain standing on the Earth. I began to soar upward as my heart swelled in my breast. I awoke with this inexplicably intense sense of Joy. Reaching for pen and paper at my bedside, I wrote the words that captured that moment of ecstasy: *"I Dance With The Stars."*

These and other events led quietly to that illuminating reading in October 1994. Yet I felt myself to be no one special, and felt quite disconnected from mainstream society. How could

I accomplish what was being presented as my destiny? My disbelief and resistance kept me paralyzed until April 14, 1996.

On this Sunday, I was compelled to sit down and type some words that were pressing in my mind and heart. My vocation as programmer/analyst caused my days to be spent in the company of about eighty people in a corporate office. The confusion, anxiety, and sadness I felt in their reactions to this work-world, and their lives in general, motivated me deeply, pushing me into action.

At the end of this writing session I printed and read what had been written. In astonishment, what I recognized on those pages was a rough draft of the Introduction, and the Chapter titles for this book. My resistance was shattered; the binder containing the rough-draft-in-progress became my constant companion. Time was found where no time existed. Lunch hours became a prime source of opportunity as words flowed forth from my heart and Spirit.

As the rough draft took shape, I found phrases and ideas gently offered into my mind. I would awake from dreams and go into my room to write what had been planted there. I would notice something at a stoplight while commuting to work, and write key phrases that would later recall the thought for further expansion. I was Lovingly guided to, and Blessed with the material that follows in these pages.

Feeling very much like a scribe as Spirit filled my Being with information for this book, I found it very fitting that the tender first rough draft was complete on December 24, 1996. My heart felt great joy and honor as this book's birth shared timing with the anniversary of Jesus' birth.

I do not have a diploma from a theological institution, nor do I have (at least in this lifetime) a depth of background in any organized church. Even a lifelong aversion to reading has held the external influence of this world's writers to a minimum in my experience.

What I do have is the knowledge that what is offered in these pages is God's Truth as received through my perception. My life has provided a neutral clean slate through which this information has resonated into existence. My openness to Spirit is simple and organic, without influence from formal religion. It has been through this creative endeavor that I have come to a profound experience of the Divine.

This book manifests my deepest dream to answer the incredible hunger I have sensed in the Heart of Humanity throughout my life. It represents my deep abiding Love for each and every one of you.

It is my heartfelt desire that these words will bring real peace and joy into you, and that you too may have that "AH HA!" experience: we all "DANCE WITH THE STARS."

Introduction

MAY I TELL YOU A STORY ABOUT LIFE? It is an exciting and magical tale that may just surprise and delight you!

Have you ever gone to a play? As you sit out front, a part of the audience, you look upon the brightly-lit stage, watching those in costume speaking lines to one another. It is like looking into a dream belonging to someone else.

Have you ever visited behind the scenes? There you see stage-hands and others in support of the production running here and there, making sure the audience sees what the director intends. Actors are poised just out of the audiences' sight, waiting for their cue to walk onto the stage and deliver their lines. It looks very different from the view out front.

What if I told you that you attend a play far more often than you might think? You may have heard the phrase: 'The whole world is a stage...' Imagine for a moment that the argument you had with your boss last week was nothing more than two actors moving through a scene you had co-authored for yourselves. The words spoken were less important than the feelings and thoughts the episode brought to your notice, less important than what was learned and carried forward.

Everything in our everyday world has convinced us that what we see is what we get. We view the world as a merciless place that thrusts experiences at us. We handle these events as best we can, and barely catch our breath before the next barrage of happenings descends upon us.

What I will ask you to contemplate is a very different world. A world in which you have more control than you ever dreamed. Imagine a world filled with wondrous mysteries with which you can learn to work in harmony. You can create for yourself a life that is comfortable, happy, even joyful.

In this book, we will investigate the reality that each of us is a spiritual Being in physical form. We are here to walk through the scenes we create for ourselves, to foster our growth. We will consider that our world is our college, where every day brings the potential of new lessons and understanding.

What will be presented in these pages will be similar to what someone would see while peeking backstage at the theater. We will learn to see our everyday world from a new and simplified perspective. Even those things we have known all our lives will yield fresh experiences.

Over the last thirty years, my interest in metaphysics and spirituality has led me on a winding journey through books, workshops and life observations. What I have absorbed has come together in me like delicious ingredients to be baked in contemplation and reflection. Well, the egg timer has sounded! The delicate pastry shell filled with the rich flavors of my understanding sits hot from the oven. I offer you a plate rimmed in gold, made of the finest china. I welcome your company as we feast together on food for the Soul. Food designed to melt the distance between us, and satisfy our hunger, as never before. All you need do is get comfortable, engage your imagination, and allow room for all possibilities.

Who Is God?

GOD IS LIKE THE EXECUTIVE PRODUCER of our Play. He oversees the production, and lovingly provides guidance to all those working in concert as the life-creation evolves. The Play would not exist without Him, although He maintains a low profile.

Before we start our quest to know God, I would like to defuse two issues around this subject.

First, our English language is poorly equipped to deal with descriptive words free from the coloration of gender. When one attempts to convey a simple idea, the need for a *"he," "she"* or *"it"* brings gender prejudices to mind. When rolling the concept of God around, the quality of the ideas shared will be more accurate if we entertain these thoughts free of gender. God encompasses ALL aspects of being, including aspects we perceive separately as male or female. Because of this shortcoming in our language, the convention used in this book will be male pronouns when one is needed.

Second, using the word "God" can lead one too easily into religious dogma. God is of Divine origin. Religions are a worldly creation. God is without affiliation, for He encompasses ALL things. To get past this human language limitation, we can substitute other terms. Such expressions as The Creator, Holy Father, Holy Spirit, Spirit, Goddess, Mother Nature, Lord, Prime Source, Central Sun, The Universe, or (my all-time favorite) Divine Oneness, conjure fewer preconceived notions, and assist in freeing our imagination from learned patterns. These and many other descriptive words bypass the mind and allow the heart to drift in childlike wonder of His majesty.

Before we start, I would like you to relax. Forget all of the explanations you have heard through the years about God. Pretend you are a five-year-old child. You are sitting on the floor as your beloved elder sits rocking in a chair before a fireplace. The warmth and golden color of the fire make your faces stand out as the flames flicker brightly. The natural love you feel for one another gently surrounds you. You feel warm and safe…

Now, let us consider! Most of us have wondered about the possibility that something or someone, outside of our immediate knowing, could be responsible for all that we see. And if so, what would this most creative Being be like? Well, given that any entity powerful enough to create our entire Cosmos just might be beyond our human imagination, we can only hope to glimpse His essence as a hazy understanding in our hearts.

The information written throughout the ages has themes in common that might give us our clues. "In the beginning there was the Word…and the Word was God." If eternity can in fact have a beginning, there was something or someone who birthed the incredibly complex Existence in which we find ourselves immersed.

For what purpose would such a Creation have been manifested? Suppose that all of it was put into motion as a wonderful experiment, a grand what-if scenario in the infinite Mind of a Supreme Being: an infinite field of expression in which Light and Dark compete for territory.

Things of a pure nature continue almost as if by perpetual motion. For example, when a tuning fork made of a fine alloy is struck, the tone emanating from it remains audible for a very long time. Its vibration carries on. Something of a more coarse nature—perhaps a cowbell—vibrates less efficiently. Its expression soon fades out to silence.

Our world and all that we see has existed (vibrated) for longer than we can imagine; and we all expect the Universe will continue *forever!* In this case, we take perpetual motion for granted. To maintain this infinity, the materials from which it is constructed must be of the purest essence: even as the Universe unfolds in its own unique way, it shows no sign of ending. A friend of mine is fond of saying, "If God ever stops humming, we are all in a lot of trouble!"

Everywhere our scientists look, there are symphonies of patterns that amaze them. It does not matter how powerful a microscope or telescope is used to examine matter. The next more powerful instrument invented finds even more pieces and parts, working together to weave the fabric of our Existence.

Much of what science observes in the physical world cannot be explained from the rational mind alone. There are too many mysterious elements that work in concert, too many connections to dismiss as coincidence. As each question gets answered, more questions always come to mind.

Even when answers are found, tomorrow's discoveries can prove them shortsighted. No, the world is not flat. No, the human body can go faster than 35 mph and survive. Our humanness limits our ability to fully comprehend the magnitude of what we examine.

Many debunkers attempt to use science to disprove the existence of God, miraculous events, or validity in metaphysical sensitivities. Yet science and spirituality have a great deal in common. They both move with the currents that exist in Creation, to synthesize new discoveries that benefit Humanity. As scientists accept *what is,* and allow their work to flow naturally from intuition coming from their hearts, they will produce revolutionary discoveries that work in harmony with Nature. Separations between areas of science are beginning to dissolve. Everyone is moving toward the understanding that all things are related, all things are One.

After looking outward into the infinity of time and space, to ponder the wonderful essence of our Dear Father, I smile warmly with the knowledge that He is as much in the center of myself as He is evidenced outside me. When I am quiet and listen to my breath with eyes closed, I begin to feel the warmth and closeness of His Love. The more I open to this endless flood of Love, the more I feel my connection with the whole of Creation, and with all living things.

God truly IS Love. This fine vibration holds our Existence gently, allowing for each of us our own expression. It is the purest, simplest tone of all: Love sweeter and loftier than can be known on this physical plane. Love of a simplistic purity that can only be glimpsed during our truly selfless moments of deep caring for others. This Love is ALWAYS unconditionally ours, and flows abundantly from Divine Oneness. Love that guarantees our every need be met, and our dreams and choices be gently supported.

If you do not feel this Love in your life, know that you can learn to do so. The Love is always there. It is your ability to allow it into your experience that needs refining. You are absolutely capable of knowing God's Love very personally and completely!

So here we are: an inseparable part of this most grand Creation of God's Love, experiencing the freedom in every moment to think, say and do what we choose. If this is true, why is there still savagery, famine and fatal illnesses? So if this God-guy is so loving, why is there so much suffering? Here is where our new perspective can bring great understanding.

Our lives and every decision we make are under our own direction. The Loving promise that we have from God is that no matter what our choices are, or where they lead us, we will always have His unconditional Love. Although He set all of Existence in motion as a wonderful playhouse for our performances, the rules by which we choose to live our lives are our creations. We have been granted Free Will.

Natural Truths make themselves known, when we truly seek them in our hearts. It does not take a genius to imagine that taking the life of another human is not a most loving act. However, whether I choose to follow this Truth in my personal choices is up to me, alone. **The Big Guy will love me as much one way or the other.**

My choices do have real repercussions. They affect the quality of my accumulated understanding and growth. They color my experience of myself, and the way I perceive my life and the world around me. The sum of my choices becomes the fabric of my personal existence.

If my choices are loving and caring, my Being becomes more divine and its vibrational frequency increases, thereby creating a feeling of joy and fulfillment. If my choices take a darker road, the vibratory frequency of my spirit decreases. My body feels heavier, and I am less happy or sure of where I find myself. The choices we make in every moment create the amount of Light or Dark making up the *Body of God*. Our individual choices cannot be separated from the Whole of Existence.

As we each create and live our life, so do all other Beings. We all join together to make up God's Creation. Our Existence can be likened to a fraternal organization, one in which all people are members. We might think of it as an Actors' Guild.

Since we have all been participating in God's club for quite some time, what do you imagine our club motto might be? I suspect it has three key words: *Love, Simplicity,* and *Light Heartedness.*

Love is the vibration that is our Existence. In our physical body, it flows into our Being through our heart. It warms the center of us, and causes great kindness to flow easily. It is the highest of expressions we can experience. It is the easy, fluid current available to us that moves just beneath the surface in every experience.

Simplicity is what we have forgotten all about. Today's Western society has made an art form of making things complicated. We create rules, techniques and methods that eat our time, but provide little of substance. We become so intent on executing the instructions accurately, we forget to notice and experience what is happening.

As complex as our Existence seems, it is through simplicity that each of us best expresses ourselves. The complexities seen by science are those things that God's creative hand has put in motion for our use. It is not important that we humans prod and examine, striving to understand the exact makeup of Existence. This framework is God's department. Our department is expressing our own true Self, within this framework provided.

This is where the simple takes over. When we act in simple ways, we engage our heart to birth our decisions, and we use our minds to help manifest the creation begun in the heart. However with complexity, we move further from beginnings fashioned in the heart. Our actions become controlled by major mental constructions, lacking any real life. Anything that requires a lengthy course of action, that *must* follow prescribed methods, is suspect.

The best way to build a complex creation is from a flow of simple actions. Everything builds on everything else. Nothing stands alone. To create a sound outcome, all actions must be taken in small increments. Once each step in a creative process is achieved, one knows the *truth* of this new position. From this current perspective, it becomes quite obvious what action is best to take next.

For example, if you are breaking ground for a skyscraper, it is usually too early to decide on the drapery fabric for the penthouse. Months later while standing in this space as construction nears completion, the appropriate color scheme and textures will flow naturally into your mind.

While living in Los Angeles, I watched the Bonaventure Hotel under construction, as I walked to the office building where I worked. So compelling was its form, that I quit my job, and hired on as a secretary with the Hotel's Sales Department to be personally involved.

When the Bonaventure opened, I was amazed at the imbalance I sensed in the large open area that welcomed guests. The strong lines and flow of the rough textured walls in this huge space overshadowed the decorations. It was far from a warm and fuzzy place to be. It took many changes, over a long period of time, to evolve into a space in which a person could sit comfortably and relax. I often suspected the original decor had come straight from artist's renderings prepared early during planning, rather than from direct experience with the building.

Approaching activities in our lives with a patient attitude, ensures our ability to stay focused and in touch with what we are creating. This allows our natural guidance to gently suggest adjustments in our approach along the way. When our heart births our decisions, our life and its creations stand soundly, gently supporting our personal truth.

The third key word, **Light Heartedness**—our sense of humor—is what keeps us on our toes and alert. Living one's life with this attitude keeps us in tune with our own true Self, and lets us express ourselves in pure simple terms. Without lightheartedness in place, we forget to observe life from a high-level overview. We lose perspective, and start becoming stuck in fragments of the whole experience. As our attention narrows, we start missing much of what is going on. Seriousness creeps in like a darkness, moving us into our minds and away from the heart.

When we forget to laugh at ourselves, we have to go through the trouble of thinking we know what we are doing. You know what a big pain trying to keep that fabrication afloat can be!

Life is meant to be easy and fun. If it feels difficult and serious, we are either putting our attention into things that have little lasting value for us, or we are viewing the situation from a poor choice of perspective. Laughter and delight are infectious elixirs that heal the spirit and open our hearts.

So here we are, every one a member in God's Club. It is far from exclusive: if you are breathing, you are a member, as are all fish and birds, creatures of the forest, the trees and rocks, the oceans and mountains, our sweet planet Earth and sun, every distant galaxy and nebula. All that we see, and are capable of perceiving, is all part of the Whole that is God.

We are Divine Oneness, and Divine Oneness is we. If you were not sure you knew who God was, be assured: He is everything you have ever known!

Life Is More
Than You Might Suspect

So HOW DID YOUR LIFE BEGIN? This life, the one you have
been living since birth on planet Earth. I want to share with you
the idea that this life is but one of many Plays you have staged
for yourself, over the centuries. You are actually a clever and
experienced playwright. Let us look at what happened before
the moment of your birth, to see what preceded what you think
of as your life. . .

Before Birth

Before our mother gives us birth, we attend production
meetings where the rough draft of our Play is sketched out. At
this time—between physical lifetimes—we are one with our
higher-self, and the contents of every past life is consciously
known. Interactions from past lifetimes are evaluated. Agreements are struck between souls to resolve any imbalances
remaining (karmic debts) in the coming incarnation. Scenarios
most conducive to the maturing of our soul are evaluated. The
underlying theme or purpose for the incarnation is decided.

Birth parents to provide the best physical vehicle for our hero are selected in meetings with higher-selves of actors already performing in the physical arena. The planetary influences are considered to decide the best timing for the birth. The primary guides who will watch over you and give assistance when asked are present. All these factors and more went into the production meetings before your birth. And you, as your Play's hero, presided at each gathering, and was the director and writer of your script.

So let us imagine we are in the planning stages of your Play. The desire to mount a production has gained momentum, and it is time to have open casting. The basic message or purpose of your Play is important to bear in mind so that the best choice of actors will be made. We have a solid script outline, and everyone is very excited with the creative energy swirling in the activity.

The story line revolves around your central character: you will live a life of a particular flavor, in a particular country. As the hero and primary playwright, you will have fascinating adventures, meeting many people.

On your path through life, your selected theme or purpose will emerge. If you are sensitive and willing, you will become consciously aware of this purpose, and begin to move in harmony with it. When this happens, most marvelous things begin to occur. Your life becomes light, fluid and joyful. Things begin to fall into place, and your life fulfills your grandest dreams in the happiest of endings.

But understand: *every Play is dynamically performed.* Although the script is written, it is but a suggested outline from which all things become possible. For each hero has been provided with free will. In every moment, he is well within his rights to choose a new direction of exploration. But no matter what choices are made, the underlying theme—recognized or not—weaves through the experiences.

So, to best provide fertile ground for our theme to emerge, what country or societal status is most appropriate? What parents will provide the best physical vehicle to support the events outlined? What family life will foster the most beneficial belief system? What major life occurrences will sweep through at crucial times to enhance what is unfolding? What other major characters will be cast, to appear and interact with our hero? So much to plan! So many logistical details to sketch into our scenes!

And just when we begin to get excited for our hero in his quest for adventure, our focus softens and broadens a bit to take in a new perspective. Every actor that signs up to participate to some degree in our Play-action, also has their own script outline, in which *they* are the heroes.

So we have Plays within Plays, overlapping and intertwining. Individuals and groups of actors discuss possible interactions that will serve each of their own story lines and growth. Good friends decide to be family members in their individual Plays, to coincide and influence one another for a while.

The broad details are discussed and finalized in these production meetings. Finally, you take your position and upon cue, move out onto the Stage into the middle of the delivery room. You utter your first sounds as you, our fresh brave hero, venture into your story line.

How does our Play work?

Of course you are not truly the "first" hero to launch into his Play. Already millions of story lines exist at various stages of expression. You add yet one more dimension to the total symphony, that is the complex dance of humanity.

As befits any actor in expression, you possess one ability or aspect that is completely unique among all actors. The world is brightened one bit more by your presence.

The process of being born is a difficult passage. We arrive with full knowledge of being One with the Whole of Creation. Once born, the noisy, glittering physical world overwhelms us. So starts the cycle of forgetting the after-world, and beginning one's body of worldly knowledge. This process turns what was Christ consciousness into a muffled haze. But this is how it must be, for the experiences in the physical world to seem *real*. It is through these "real" experiences that the actor grows and matures.

Our ego forms to make rational sense out of the avalanche of information. As our Being transitions into the physical, worldly habits and beliefs are established. The true dynamics at work, forming the world we experience, become hidden from us.

So how can all of this work? What if I decide to go to Harvard instead of Yale? What happens to those actors ready for interaction when I do not arrive? Well, everyone's story line adjusts—it is dynamic (I told you.) It is not the explicit who and where, as much as the quality of the experiences through which one moves. Besides, if it is really important that you make connection with a particular person, you will. I met the man I married when sent to Newark, New Jersey by my employer. I was living in Los Angeles at the time, while preparing to move to Houston. I did not have a chance! Nor did he.

As you may begin to suspect, more Beings actually exist behind the scenes, making the details come together, than there are actors on the Stage. All that talk about guardian angels, guides, and being watched over, is as real as the coffee mug you hold in the morning. We are all members of the same Actors' Guild. However while we hang out in the third dimension on Mother Earth, our guides do their things in the higher vibrational dimensions. No wonder it is a bit difficult to prove their existence using our third-dimensional instrumentation.

If you are beginning to get the feeling of a crowd, your imagination is taking you in the right direction. For myself, it is impossible to ever feel alone.

Coming to know what I am sharing with you as your own truth can be difficult. For awhile, these ideas will be no more than words heard in your mind. It will take personal experience with these ideas in your life, before they become a real part of you. The difficulty in believing this broader perspective is a tribute to the perfect workings of our physical framework, provided by our dear Executive Producer.

As an actor in your current Play, it is important that you stay in character to gain full benefit from that which unfolds. If you had full memory of your many past lifetimes, this would be difficult. Consider the following: an actor in a theater on Earth must stay in character for the play to have meaning. If such an actor were suddenly distracted by the thought that his rent was due the following day, he would slip out-of-phase with his character, and the play would lose its impact at that moment. In the same way, if you had perfect recall of all of your previous lives, and the divine existence between those lifetimes, you could not stay in character. It would be difficult for you to move through your script, or to learn and grow through the experiences. You would want to remove your makeup, and go Home, to relax with divine friends.

Although full knowledge of the Divine is not possible in our physical form, we can become more sensitive to its rhythm. The more sure I become of life's hidden activity, the more closely I watch for each subtle nuance within that which unfolds; and the more FUN life becomes! Although the world's perfect illusion provides a solid appearance, I am constantly tantalized to seek out its hidden aspects, and read between its lines. What I experience more every day is a sense of excitement and adventure.

Being here in physical form accomplishes more than just satisfying our own story lines. We are all together, playing out this complex, dynamic interaction of individual Plays. We are as much here to support others in their scripts, as we are to express our own. So the idea of service to others in this world is as natural as taking a breath. Not the ego-based "I volunteer four more hours a week than you do (nah-na-nah-nah)" stuff, but the moment-to-moment interactions that flow effortlessly between actors.

Regardless of what is commonly accepted, we are spiritual Beings. Our souls come here to have experiences in the physical, so we can grow and evolve to a more enlightened state. Our body, with all of its delightful senses, is our vehicle designed to facilitate this learning. All of us, interacting together, form a total consciousness for humanity on Earth. Even this body of humanity as a whole has an overall essence with lessons to learn and growth to accomplish.

Our growth cannot be considered separately from all other living creatures on Earth, or separately from our planet itself. Even this beautiful globe, hurling through space, moves toward a perfect expression of the most that she can be. We are all interwoven into the Whole that includes every perceivable part and parcel of Existence, the Whole that is God's Creation, God Himself.

Between lifetimes, we exist in a divine, angelic form—our higher-self—and live entirely within God's Loving presence. When we are born into the physical to experience our Play, the soul that inhabits our body is a fragment from this Whole. It is as if our higher-self slips his foot into a slipper to walk upon our planet. This slipper is our physical body. Our higher-self receives the benefit of the experiences in our life, and thereby achieves growth.

One morning as I opened my eyes from meditation, I experienced a unique physical sensation that lasted for about forty-five seconds. I had been feeling grateful to my higher-self and guides, for their support in my life. As I moved my arm to rise from the chair, I had the sensation of many arms moving. As I focused on this sensation, I felt hundreds of bodies within mine, mimicking the movements I made. In a moment of understanding, I knew I was feeling all the physical forms I had inhabited in other lifetimes, in other Plays. All of these bodies, previously born, were superimposed within my current form.

I was amazed to have this massive expanse of lifetimes focused within my senses in one moment.

So we have our physical form, as well as our more subtle divine higher-self, guides, and angels. Information can flow into our consciousness from these Beings, as we learn to tune into the subtle wavelength connecting us. This communication can be noticed as those thoughts that suddenly pop into our minds. Perhaps a thought to phone someone we have not talked to in sometime, or a sudden desire to stop at a roadside fruit stand where you meet a new dear friend, or perhaps just a reminder "don't forget your lunch" as you open the door to leave. These suggestions are just that. Whether we follow them or not is within our own choosing—free will is our greatest gift!

The Ego

During early life, we forget from where we have just come, and are taught the world's accepted methods of behaving. We develop certain worldly aspects that include things like ego, our desire to control our lives, and a wide assortment of fears that can haunt us at every turn.

Initially, the ego serves as a safe buffer between the garish, coarse physical world, and the soft gentle inner spiritual Being. It is actually a protective mechanism, constructed by the young actor's mind as he is bombarded with how-tos, when-tos and why-nots, by those humans older than himself.

To our young mind, the myriad of instructions presented by those people, able to quench our young physical hunger and thirst, *must* express the truth. They have survived this odd physical existence so foreign to one just arrived. So all these instructions and "truths" are stored away in our most wonderful mind. Soon, Mr. Ego comes on the scene to take charge of organizing and accessing all this stored information. He becomes central and quite important, if he may say so himself.

When a playmate is mean, our ego chimes in, "Suzie is ten times more stupid than she says we are. Give her a push down, and we'll go find someone clever to play with." You can just imagine the chaos going on when young children are playing together. Each child's ego going through formative stages, struggling to get this new physical creature stabilized into a superlative person. All the time gathering more words of wisdom from the adults, the ego tries to work these new ideas in with what has been heard before, so that it all makes sense.

Take a few minutes, close your eyes and quiet your mind. Focus on listening to your breath, or pretend in your mind's eye you are looking at an empty chalkboard and focus your attention on it. See how long it takes before your chattering mind distracts you: this is your ego.

Your ego does not want you to connect with your inner world. Your ego knows that to be quiet, and to empty one's mind, is to allow those simple ideas to flow in from your heart, from your higher-self, from Spirit. If you get comfortable taking your directions from a Divine source, he is out of a job. Mr. Ego says, "Can't have that, this person couldn't survive without me."

Do not believe this! Such thoughts are your ego's scare tactics. We are so accustomed to our ego pushing us around, that we erroneously assume the little voice dominating our conscious mind to be who we are.

Our egos are like little Napoleons who have taken over and seem to have a life of their own. The ego, in strongest terms, is your physical form in expression without intervention from Spirit. It operates out of the mind, and rarely listens to the heart. The heart is the source from which loving, divine thoughts flow naturally into the conscious mind.

The ego is ever watchful for ways its powers might be diminished. Listening openly to gentle thoughts from the heart, sends cold shivers down its back. It hustles to fill the conscious mind with babbling dialogue that drowns out the simple thoughts from Higher places.

All of this mental activity is just that. It makes judgments about issues based wholly on what someone said about it. Operating from the ego is putting all of one's eggs in a third-dimensional basket. It is the rare child that finds his center, and challenges ideas thrust at him based on how they *feel* to him. It can take a very long time for a human to understand they can question whether something offered is really true for themselves.

The ego does not readily accept Spiritual ideas. It may take a fancy to a religious organization with all of its important persons and business going on, but personal quiet spiritual communing is not on the agenda. Instead, the ego views most events in our life as unexpected dangerous stuff, that must be controlled or avoided. Our ego does not accept that the scenes of our Play are created by ourselves to facilitate our own growth. No, Mr. Ego takes no responsibility for our haphazard path through life.

With little practice, you can become confident in your ability to know the source of an idea. Did it come from your worldly based ego, or did it come from your higher-self or Spirit? If it comes expressed in forceful or critical words, bubbling with emotions, you can bet old Mr. Ego has climbed up on his high horse again. However, if the idea is gentle and quiet, with simple words, you will know it did not come from your ego.

You can test any thought by examining it with your heart. If the idea feels cold and sterile, yup Mr. Ego is at work. If your heart warms and the idea seems to swell, increasing in size, then you have an idea which contains personal value, something well worth exploring further.

Here is another sure clue to identifying your ego's activity. Have you ever found conflicting opinions in yourself about something? Perhaps you discovered a conflict by coming at a subject from two different angles. When this happens, you have noticed the flawed work of your ego. There is so much information from so many different human sources that unresolved differences have to exist.

When these differences begin to give you reason for concern, there are two solutions: (1) ignore them (*being asleep*), or (2) begin to question why such a thing could happen, and begin testing the conflicting ideas against what feels right in your heart (*being awakened*). Once you are using your own essence-vibration as the yardstick against which all ideas are measured, there will *not* be varying opinions. You always know how an idea *feels* to you. Your truth is your truth. It may evolve throughout your life, but in any given moment it is stable. Ask your heart, and let your higher-self guide you to your solid conclusion.

The first step to take your life back, and dissolve the ego, is to become consciously aware of what you think, say and do. When you live in a state of conscious awareness, you will achieve the most growth possible.

In every moment, you make decisions about what to do or say next. Begin to notice the evaluation process you use to make these choices. How much is simply habit? If you find yourself just doing what you have always done, without feeling whether it is still right for you, then **congratulations:** you are consciously *noticing* what you are doing. This is the first necessary step before you can choose to change it. You are on your way to becoming a consciously awakened Human Being.

This process takes time. Habits are stubborn, and your ego will be throwing up objections and flooding you with stray ideas to distract you from your quest. Your ego will activate your most personal fears in an attempt to regain control over your thoughts and intentions. When this happens, realize you are *noticing* the dynamics going on in your mind. Again, realize your progress toward a new life of conscious awareness. Praise yourself for loosening the grip of your ego.

So, if your Play seems dull and predictable, let me assure you: you are asleep. Your time here guarantees to be an exciting flow of vignettes: each introduces the next. All you must do is become consciously aware of your choices, and lull Mr. Ego to sleep. If you think you know who you are and where you are going, but your ego still has you by the throat, then you have some surprises coming when you surrender to your natural process.

Forgiveness and Acceptance

As you practice this new way of being, you will find you can easily become your own most harsh critic. Instead of focusing on what you perceive as poor choices, understand you are making wonderful headway. You are *noticing* what you are doing. You cannot truly begin to sense the primary theme in your Play, until you consciously evaluate your life in each moment, as it flows along.

As you learn to do this, you will have plenty of opportunity to practice forgiveness. It is most important to forgive yourself any perceived shortcomings. Forgiveness detaches the control that negative emotions can exert on you. Even though you are a spiritual Being, you must learn to be gentle and loving with your physical self.

Your mind, body and soul are perceived as a solid physical form. But this "body" is actually vibrating molecules through which electromagnetic energy flows. To work most efficiently, the energy moving in your body needs to flow freely, without restriction. The way you *feel about yourself* actually affects this flow of energy. Through forgiveness, energy blocked from flowing freely, or energy consumed by holding ill feelings, can be released to feed and support positive aspects in your life.

To release blocked energy in your body, and bring a new sense of freedom into your life, try saying the following aloud:

> *I forgive myself, and all others, for any hurt or harm experienced. I release any feelings I hold from these past injuries. I feel calmness flowing into my mind. I feel my tense muscles relax, and I breathe deeply of the peaceful*

air. Thank you, dear Self, for your courage to let go of what has been known, to allow space for our new adventure in the unknown.

If a situation or experience comes into your life that causes you pain, look at it closely. Most often it is replaying something that occurred previously: either in this or another lifetime. It has come forward to give you another chance to treat it differently than in the past. It is offering you the opportunity to handle it from your heart. Once recognized, you can forgive and release the trapped energy in your body, that is sustaining a cellular memory of this hurt. You can forgive, and let it go.

No pattern recurs in your life to bring you pain. It comes to you so you can move consciously through it, and release its affect from your life. It comes offering you a self-healing, that only you can provide. It challenges you to become very aware of the symbolic messages unfolding in your life, and to only be receptive to those elements you find positive in nature. If you find nothing of value in something from your current vantage point, walk away. You owe no one any explanations. Being true to yourself is all the reason you need.

Handling yourself gently, with love and forgiveness, is how life is meant to be lived. By loving and forgiving yourself, you are left without burdens as you move on in your life. Once you become able to forgive yourself, this ability naturally transfers to those around you. Practicing forgiveness brings a deep level of freedom. Your way becomes far easier.

As you learn to forgive and release negative feelings, you will find a position of acceptance will move into you. You will begin to see those around you as the actors they are. You will understand, and allow them the quest of their own story line. Things they do or say will impact you less directly.

When you accept others as a unique aspect of God in expression, you will find you can love them far more easily. They are your brothers and sisters. Even when they make a decision in their life that mystifies you, it is their own story line they are designing. Your understanding is not necessary. Freely allow them their own direction. They deserve your love and acceptance.

Universal Laws and Our Creative Ability

Many dynamics are at your disposal to shape your life. They are in effect whether you recognize them or not. The amazing truth is: *to the finest detail, each of us creates the quality of our life, and chooses how we perceive it.* **We create our own reality.**

Likes attract likes. Opposites, or things out of harmony with one another, repel each other. This is a Universal law of energy. If you become consumed with anger, you will find yourself in cranky situations with surly individuals. If you are accepting of others, and do not hold ill feelings, you will find your world filled mostly with congenial people.

Decisions you make **change** *your life.* For example, you may choose to release some feelings or thoughts because you perceive them as negative or contrary to your growth. When you forgive and release these things, you are changing the complexion of your world. You will find yourself no longer wanting to spend time with actors still holding the thought you have released. You will simply not feel comfortable with them. At the same time, you will begin meeting people who share your new point of view.

From your personal perspective, the external world reflects the current condition of your inner world. The law of like energies attracts to you, and moves you among, similar energies. You create for yourself life events to experience your current lesson material. How you interpret what is happening in your life reflects the level to which you are consciously aware.

Everyone you meet acts as a mirror to show you your own strengths and weaknesses. Drawn together as like energies, we provide this service for one another. When you see something in someone you admire, you are consciously focusing on an aspect of yourself that may be ready to be expressed. Take careful notice of people with whom you interact. Watch for new insights into yourself based on your observations of others.

As spiritual souls living in the physical world, we are powerfully creative Beings. Every creation in our life starts as a thought-form. When we think a new thought, it begins to take an amorphous shape in the etheric realm. The idea hangs around in our aura—that space immediately surrounding our physical body. If the thought recurs in our conscious mind, we feed the thought-form a bit more energy, and it grows in its potential to go from thought to physical manifestation. The expression, "Be careful what you wish for…" is referring to this process.

We can control the things that manifest in our lives by consciously managing the ideas about which we think. If a thought comes into your mind that you do not approve of, tell it "No!" and push it out. Just do not give it time—think of something else. If the thought does not have a home in your mind, it cannot stay and become manifest.

We can also use our thoughts to enhance the quality of our life. When you think of something that brings you happiness or peace, take note of what it is. Perhaps you imagine a trip to the beach, or a vacation in the mountains. Then, at another time, when a stressful situation has you tense and anxious, do some deep breathing and recall your warm thought-friends. Flood your mind with the pleasant memory until there is no room for what was there. Just forget where you are, or what you are doing (it will wait for you).

As soon as you succeed in swapping your mental focus, you will come back into synch with your natural Self. You will notice a physical change in your body: it will relax, while your blood pressure and pulse rate will decline. You are creating for yourself an oasis that is gentle and supportive of the real YOU.

Thinking a thought gives it some of your energy. Speaking words aloud is tenfold stronger. Without realizing it, you can use words unwisely. You might say, "This job is going to kill me!" If you do not find yourself dead at your desk, you may experience deteriorating health. If nothing else, you will have wasted time and energy better used for creations truly wanted.

Experiment with consciously using the power of creating with words. Find something you would like to create, and say it aloud. Use clear words so your intention cannot be misunderstood. Try several ways of saying it until you come across the one that *feels* best. The phrase you select will seem to have a life of its own. When you find one that you like, say it often in your private moments, for example, "*Unnecessary fat in my physical body melts and flows back to the Universe.*"

After you have said your phrase enough times (you will feel done), just let it go and focus your mind on other matters. Releasing simple clear requests into the ethers can bring surprising results. If it does not happen quickly, know that the time is not yet right: it would not fit into the current time frame of your Play. Remember: your higher-self is the other half of the author. Script changes must get your higher-self's endorsement to move forward rapidly.

Make these requests to the Universe open-ended. Just state the essence of the results wanted. Do not spell out how it should happen. If you say, "I will get a raise by the end of June." it can be more limiting than you might imagine. You do not want to rule out the possibility of winning the lottery; and an earthquake, causing your home to push twenty feet into the air, probably was not what you meant either. Instead, say something like, "*My financial obligations are always satisfied with ease and grace.*"

The orchestration of Creation is very literal. Choose your words for the clarity with which they convey your meaning. As few words as possible—keep it simple—but say what you mean. As you say your phrases, have confidence in the creative process you are initiating. It is best to keep them private. Sharing them with someone who laughs at your "silly ideas" will do little to support its life, or bolster your feelings and intentions about the request.

If you come up with a few good ones, write them down for future reference. You will probably stop feeling a need to say them after sometime (a few days, few weeks, few months). Put the piece of paper somewhere you will find it later. You may be surprised at how they were interpreted and delivered into your life.

Once I wrote down qualities that I would like to have in the place I live. One of the statements I had written asked to "...live in a place with clear waters..." The next place we moved was to Clearwater, Florida. When I discovered the sheet of paper while unpacking, I had to laugh at the literalness with which my statement had manifested. In your co-creation process, you and the Universe can come up with some unusual solutions to requests. Always expect the unexpected, and you will not be disappointed!

If you are having difficulties in your life, use these phrases to bridge to a new way of being. You need not be specific about what to change—you may not know. Just put words together until they say what it is you would like to achieve, for example, "*I clearly feel my direction. My life flows naturally and all things are accomplished easily and at the right time.*"

Words are things. They each have their own vibration. Putting words together to sing the song of your desires has great creative power.

Symbols

Nothing is as serious as we tend to make it. This can be a difficult idea to grasp and integrate into one's life. Remember that you are simply in a Play. We are "play"ing with one another using the physical realm rules of gravity, centrifugal force, etc. What is important is the behind-the-scenes activity, and our quest to come into harmony with our Play's theme or purpose.

When occurrences in our life are evaluated in pure spiritual terms, they never seem serious. They just are. As we begin to recognize the true purpose of our life, our understanding around it is calm and warm. It is cloaked in love and light. If our life seems perpetually serious or difficult, we are simply off track.

Even though the life situations you create for yourself seem to play-out in the physical world, they are actually designed to work through issues at focus in your inner, Spiritual world. The energies in action are symbolic of the current area of your soul's growth. With practice, you can begin to read between the lines of your life's patterns. You will begin to understand what lesson you are asking yourself to learn and accept. There are yummy little clues in every person your eyes meet, and every situation that unfolds. What we all believe to be a rock-solid reality, takes on great waves of surrealism after you tune into the symbols flying by. When you become consciously aware of your Play, life can become quite fun.

What I mean by symbols is the hidden meaning in events that occur. Some general examples follow, however realize the examples I am sharing with you are how I have interpreted these symbols. The same event in your life may bring very different representations to your mind.

Imagine you forget for a moment that such things can hurt, and you touch the handle of a hot pan on the stove and burn your finger. You may wish you had not done so and rush to grab the coolness of an ice cube, but why did this happen? This event has drawn your attention to the fingers of your dominant hand. It (as with all things) has happened for a reason. Soften your attention, and allow this feeling in your hand to play with your imagination. Watch for what ideas come to your mind. Is there a situation in your life where you are *handling* things a bit too insensitively, without your full attention? Are you causing unexpected pain to someone by your actions?

If a thought comes to you when you focus your attention in this way, allow it to lead you to a new understanding. Have patience with yourself. You are learning to discern subtle messages.

The trick here is to discriminate between the voice of ego, and the voice of Spirit. With practice, using some of the techniques discussed earlier to spot the ego's activities, the voice of Spirit becomes the dominant thought. When you evaluate a situation in this way, you actually experience a *sensation of knowing*: the symbol delivers its message into your mind.

Another constant source of personal information is your automobile. The vehicle you use for transportation symbolized an extension of your own physical body. The basic condition of your car, and any mechanical difficulties you experience, can provide great personal insight.

If your starter gives you trouble, you may well find resistance to *getting started* in some necessary activity in your life. If you get a speeding ticket, you may be asking yourself to *slow down*, or to *stop forcing forward* into your life activities. If your transmission is slipping, you may find you are inconsistent in the way you *engage your energy* in your daily activities.

Symbols you translate may represent relatively small issues in your life, or you may uncover a major idea that allows you to jell the past five years of your life into a new perspective. Until you look into them, you will not know how significant they are. As you work with discovering hidden meanings in your life events, your familiarity with how you use symbols will increase. Getting guidance from an event will become easier.

Although it may seem otherwise, life is a flowing continuum. Nothing is unrelated. All things are One. As you tune into the symbology in your life's situations, the relationship between very different events will begin to occur to you. The thread or pattern weaving through the events will become more clear.

I was leaving a job I had in Houston. On the way to work that last morning, the traffic was impossible. Cars were pushing in everywhere, and it was much more stop than go. I was thinking about the young man I had trained as my replacement, and the meeting we were both attending in thirty minutes with the computer steering committee. I was consumed with ways in which I could guide him to handle the discussion issues the best way. I could feel my desire to influence his decisions. Suddenly, I stopped. I realized I had trained him well. This was my last day. His methods of handling the meeting were not mine to define. I was merely there to answer questions, if asked. This situation was moving out of my script and into his.

As soon as I understood and *accepted* my real place in the forthcoming event, I could not believe my eyes. Every car in front of me started turning off the road. Every resistance I had experienced blocking my forward movement simply moved aside. Traffic got up to speed and I arrived at work with no further delays. I was being told very clearly that when my ego released control, I had stepped into the correct mindset.

The Subtle Realms

As you bravely open to the possibility of subtle information in your life, you will begin to experience ideas that seem odd indeed. In fact, the more you open to the unknown, the more odd occurrences, ideas and coincidental happenings will come to your notice. If you hear a noise in the next room and you know no one is there, do not quickly dismiss it. Instead of convincing yourself you are hearing things, you might wonder who is playing with you from beyond your normal senses.

When it comes to entities from beyond our physical world, know right now: nothing other than what you truly want to occur can happen. **You** are the creator of your personal reality. Nothing harmful can come through and bother you *if you do not want it to.* Any entity interested in communicating with you must get your permission to interact. Much of this will occur on a subconscious level, but your higher-self will be very aware of any agreements or permissions given. You have complete control over your domain. If you are uncomfortable, say aloud, *"Only those Beings of the Highest Good are welcome in my presence. All others, be gone, NOW!"* And it is so.

You see, each of us is an incredibly powerful Being. We have been given free will, with total co-creative privileges to design our own life. There are no victims. There are only agreements between actors to interact in a general scenario, for a particular reason. You may agree to meet to resolve an imbalance from a previous life interaction, or to provide a format in which a lesson can be experienced to provide growth. On a subconscious level, in full agreement with your higher-self, you always control the flow of your story line.

Information flows into your heart and mind from your higher-self and guides. These Beings have little better to do than keep an eye on what is happening in your Play. It is their service to you, given freely with great love.

Since many of us are overly critical of ourselves, we may not feel worthy of full-time attention from others. But despite this limiting opinion, we are lovingly helped by Beings from beyond the physical—from the other side of the Veil. To them, their service to us is a joy and honor. In their chosen profession as guide, they help orchestrate the refinement of the total expression of Creation through their guidance given to us.

This access to knowledge from *beyond* is naturally a part of each of us. It is not unusual for people to experience receiving information in the form of premonitions. Perhaps you think "my mother is going to phone" and the telephone rings; or you feel in your bones your young child is in mischief, and you arrive in the other room just before that golf tee is swallowed.

In my early twenties, I had a premonition I was going to hit someone with my car. So abhorrent was this thought that I could not believe there could be truth in it. Yet the thought persisted. About a month and a half after the first occurrence of this thought, I was driving my 1955 Chevrolet panel truck down a hill to an intersection. As I approached, the traffic light turned green, and I rolled into the intersection to make my left turn. The thought of "bone on fender" burst *loudly* into my mind.

I slowed and moved my head to the side. To my surprise, a young college student was walking toward me in the crosswalk. She was engrossed in a book, paying no attention to the sparse traffic. Her movement and my turning were synchronized, so that she had been hidden from my view by the tall side mirror on the truck. I simply slowed and she walked on, never realizing the impending incident in her Play would not occur. From that moment on, the feeling was gone and has never recurred.

I now understand this potential automotive accident was an agreement struck between our two souls. From the care with which I was guided to avoid consummating the contract, I know the lesson involved was no longer needed, or appropriate, in my script. However if the young college student still needed such an experience in her script, wheels were already in motion to find another actor with whom to set up the revised scene.

What we do in the physical world is more than just exercising our own creative expression in our script. The degree to which growth can occur is very concentrated while in physical form. As we are nudged this way and that, by our dear friends from beyond, our personal growth brings our being to a more enlightened state. As our personal essence evolves, our vibration increases: it affects everyone and everything throughout Creation.

Crossroads

From our original script, there are *"doors of opportunity"* that become available in our lives at different times. Also, actions taken during our life can set up circumstances that will create a new doorway in our future. Imagine feeling completely blocked in your job, and then your phone rings. Someone you had met through a professional organization is starting a new department in their company, and your face came into their mind. So they call you. Is this just a coincidence? I think not!

At some point, an agreement was struck between your two higher-selves to work closely together. The blockage experienced in your current job was simply the completion of your forward movement in the old situation. This ending made room for the new opportunity to pop in. One of your doors of opportunity opened right up, and put out the welcome mat. However, it is your free will to choose to step through or not.

Our life's progression is like traveling a maze. When an opportunity door presents itself, we either accept and pass through, or we choose not to enter, and it is gone. These doorways may be events, relationships, a change in personal attitude, anything that will bring with it a new set of experiences. As we select which opportunities to accept, our script dynamically adjusts to the new setting. The unseen Beings and natural Universal laws swing into action to support our revised path, no matter where it may lead.

If a doorway represents something important or significant to our script's theme, our higher-self will encourage us to step through. If we sidestep it, the opportunity will reappear at various times in our life, cloaked differently. If we continue to ignore it, and it is truly important for our development, we can find every other avenue in our life being shut down with delays and frustrations. Finally, even the most stubborn actor will accept and step through the opportunity's doorway, so growth can occur.

Earlier in my life, a fear of being without money was a personal obstacle. My life vignettes offered opportunities in which I could learn to release this fear, and live with trust. As long as I refused to learn this lesson, the pattern repeated and became more severe. Finally, through an odd chain of events, my husband, Lee, and I found ourselves out of work and filing for bankruptcy. (The shame our society casts on those experiencing financial difficulty makes one pause to examine exactly where our world's values are set. It is commonly thought that people who do not own things have no value themselves. However, the same person with $100,000 in the bank is considered an upstanding citizen.)

As I surrendered to the situation, and accepted the doors of opportunity as they were offered, I was constantly amazed at the synchronicity that emerged. Just as the rent was about to be overdue, a piece of furniture would sell to an unexpected visitor to make up the difference. Just as the food supply got tenuous, an odd job would come available to finance the trip to the grocery store. Although we were often down to under $20 to our names, all things needed were provided in some way. Often, the solutions were far different from anything I could have forecast.

Now I know money is a form of energy used in exchanges. It is an energy that thrives on movement. Hoarding and grasping it tightly tends to stifle the flow. If one's intentions are based in love, and free from manipulative schemes, there is always more than enough coming in to replace the outgoing flow. In fact if money is expected, it will arrive!

All decisions in your life that mark a choice of direction are doorways: What vocation attracts you? For whom will you work? Where will you move? These are questions that come forward for evaluation when an opportunity for change catches your notice.

Time and Healing

You may well be surprised as you develop a new sense about time, and how long it takes to accomplish things. For example, if you have lived many years with a psychological problem, you are encouraged to start visiting a professional counselor. The intent is for this person to listen, and help you come to an understanding of what has caused your problem. Their insight can help you to get in touch with hidden aspects of yourself. However, it is commonly thought that this process can take a very long time.

As you begin to experience yourself as a unique aspect of God in expression, you will begin to find very personal and creative ways of using your power to heal yourself. You will find no rules around how long it takes to become free of something. If you are attending sessions with a professional, you can both enjoy and learn from the speed with which your transition to health can occur.

If there is something you no longer wish to have as a part of you, identify it. Imagine what it has symbolized for you. How does it make you feel? Do you remember other experiences in your life that made you feel this way? Review the growth these experiences provided in your script. To effectively release this "something," you will actually feel love for it, and appreciate the purpose it once served, when it was appropriate in your script. You can then release it with thanks, and move on without it. You can heal yourself—*quickly*—and more simply than our modern medical science accepts as possible.

Our doctors really do not know how our bodies or brains work. Remember that this is God's area of expertise. It is beyond our human ability to understand all of the workings of our physical form. Our doctors only know which technique has been statistically proven to ease a particular observed condition. They treat a patient from the point-of-view of someone in the audience looking at an actor on the stage. Your approach will be more effective, since you know the actor in the costume.

It is not important to understand with your mind the under-lying reason for everything. Since the fabric of WHAT IS is constantly changing, adapting as your script evolves, it is not always necessary to reconstruct an earlier life perspective as part of a cure to your current condition. Also, you will rarely rid yourself of an identified "dis-ease," if its purpose within a partic-ular lesson in your life has not yet yielded its maximum value.

Often, the value provided by an illness is found in the events that occur while you work through it, to a whole and healthy condition. These words can sound hollow to someone experi-encing a serious illness. Even when one accepts responsibility for his reality, the road to self-healing can lead through valleys of disillusionment and doubt. It is difficult to trust in the midst of pain that God's Plan and your Play are linked.

Patience and Willingness

This is a fine time to recognize patience as one of our most necessary attributes. Impatience is worn like a badge of courage by many in our runaway life styles of the 1990s. However, it is only by having patience with the speed with which life events unfold, that our true purpose can begin to emerge.

Purposefully changing your own rhythm to agree with another's schedule, shifts you out of synchronization with your true Self. You can no longer recognize the symbols on your own path. If the time frames you are asked to adhere to do not feel right to you, break away. If the life rhythm does not feel right to you, it is not yours.

When you find your patience being tested, try shifting into a new point of view. Your will—your choices—are being thwarted. This is a wake up call to sit back and look around. Reevaluate where your choices are taking you. Is it really best for you? Even if your direction is sound, have you slipped into a more automatic mode, losing your conscious awareness? Something is not quite right, or you would not be feeling impatient.

It could even be as simple as you have started to become too serious. Next time you toss a crumpled piece of paper at the wastebasket, and it does a three-object ricochet to bounce back at your feet, do not get angry. Laugh at the humor with which the Universe gives you little loving nudges to push you back on track.

Many times when you feel impatient, you are not recognizing that the delays you perceive are really the ending of a phase in your life. Space must be made before new beginnings can make an appearance. If you forcibly push to make things happen, you can disrupt the natural flow of what is afoot. Recognize that divine timing (not human timing) will provide your finest opportunities.

As you begin to practice patience in your life, you will assume a position of willingness. When you are willing to fully experience events you create for yourself, as they naturally unfold, your life will begin to move more quickly. You will find that by embracing what occurs without resistance, the value in the events will flow into your core. The speed of your growth will increase. You will become synchronized with the natural flow of your life.

Perspective

An actor views a situation in which he participates from his own unique perspective. The experience unfolds to exercise lesson issues in which each participant is currently involved. Since what each actor experiences is his own interpretation of the symbols he recognizes, it is not difficult to see why different stories of what happened can be told.

When you hear a news broadcast or watch a trial on television, the stories that describe the incident can be so varied, that it appears more likely each observer was somewhere different. *Everyone's experience is UNIQUE.* When you begin to know this as truth, it becomes a wonder that any two people can ever find agreement!

History is accepted as it is because the events were written down, and thus made static. If you had been present, you would most likely disagree with the historical account.

You can only fully know your own perspective. You cannot know why another actor makes particular choices. They are living from their own perspective, following the inclinations fostered by their own story line.

Sometimes it is tempting to imagine their reasons. Perhaps you form a judgment of their action from your own perspective. But these activities do not serve your growth. Spending time this way just postpones living your own life. Why or what others say or do does not directly affect you. It is your own choices that create your direction.

Clear communication between actors is truly an art form. You must translate your perspective into words that the other person will understand as you intend. Even then, the other person will extract a meaning from your words that is personally appropriate. Once you have offered the words, your responsibility ends. How the other person chooses to perceive your words is the other half of the transaction.

Even the words in this book are written for only part of the population. Many will find no sense in them. Those actors drawn to these words are at a point of coming into a new level of conscious awareness. They thirst for something that will encourage their own forgotten knowledge into their conscious mind. If it is not words on this page, it will be something else. They are on a quest.

As your choices of what you do in each moment begin to flow more naturally, the answers you seek will flow from your inner world and be recognized by your heart. The answers will most likely come in the flavors of events as your life unfolds. You are becoming truly alive. It is a wonderful day on planet Earth!

Our Body

As spiritual Beings at Play in the physical, we are an inseparable part of Creation. Once you become aware of your natural and constant connection to all things, your body takes on a new world of sensations. You will feel your body more completely and intimately than ever before. Once you notice and examine these feelings, they become guide posts that help you know when you have lost your perspective as a spiritual Being, and have slipped back into the physical.

As you begin to know your body as something independent from YOU, you will understand YOU are not limited to the confines of its physical form. It is the physical container for your actor's essence. It surrounds you and carries you to those destinations you choose. Without it, your curtain can come down quite abruptly!

As you develop the sensation of being carried by this physical vessel, you begin to identify with being "in" a certain area of your body. Most people associate with being in their head. This is where our brain is located; it is also from this physical perspective that we view the world if we are sighted. The real person—the consciousness or soul—can move quite independently in relation to the body.

A good relaxation technique for inducing sleep can give you some experience with this idea. Get comfortable and lie on your back. Starting with your feet, slowly concentrate on each portion of your body. The object is to feel for any tension, relax the muscles, and move on to the next area until finally reaching the head. If you do not rush, and breathe deeply while quieting your mind, you will be off to dreamland well before you finish your trip.

The human way to do this is to "look down" at your feet from your head and begin. Next time, *go* to your feet. Be there and start the exercise. Do not worry about "How do I get there?" Just BE there. Be in your big toe or ball of your foot. See the toe nails right in front of you, and feel the muscles and bones surrounding you. Then request and feel the muscles around you relax.

Move up to the calf of your leg. Stroll there or just be there, whichever feels right for your consciousness as it moves to the next stop on your relaxation journey. If you drop the skepticism and try it, it will feel very real to you. You see, your consciousness knows how to travel easily without restriction. Your beliefs about yourself are what habitually locate you in your head.

Another wonderful place to visit is the heart area. It is through this energy center that thoughts, ideas and divine Love flow into us. A warm and loving quality radiates from this area. It is always available to revitalize us.

When one speaks of being centered, it can be experienced as literally placing the conscious YOU in the center of your body, just below the navel. It is a neutral place where fearful thoughts lodged in the head no longer seem valid. Such disquieting ideas lose their control and become unimportant.

Another interesting energy center to visit is at the throat. This is where spoken words emanate. If you have difficulty saying what you want to say, you will probably find tension or a sensation of lumps or blockages here. Be in the throat and promise to allow words that arise to be spoken more easily: this can help heal your self-imposed restriction.

The most dangerous place to hang out is in the head. This is where your ego makes his home. It is where you are flooded with an endless babble of unimportant thoughts, which limit your perspective of your life. It is from here that you look down at your body as if it is some foreign mystery belonging to someone else. Doctors become your interpreters to understanding its needs and weaknesses.

Your body is one of the most precious gifts you give yourself. Even if you are paralyzed from the waist down, remember: you selected your own situation before being born. The body that you have is what best allows for the growth you intended in this lifetime. Appreciate it. Tell it you love it. Mean it when you say the words. This electromagnetic complexity is a most miraculous accomplishment. Treat it as you would a best friend with thoughtfulness and love. Beginning to see your physical form in this way will help you dissolve negative habits around caring for your body. And it will not be a forced change, it will simply happen.

Feelings and Emotions

Feelings and emotions are not the same. Feelings are sensations that come to our notice as messengers from the body. They call our attention to something it is time to evaluate. We do not consciously initiate a feeling. On the other hand, we create our emotions. Emotions are synthesized as our mind works with memories and thoughts.

For example, pretend you are evaluating the pain after a slip and fall on a wet floor. You might become angry at the person who had damp mopped the floor. The pain (feeling) came as a natural result of an action you took. Your anger (emotion) only exists because you made the choice to create it. You could just as easily have chosen to take responsibility, understand and forgive.

To be consciously aware, we must learn to openly experience those feelings brought out by events in our life. Examining our feelings gives us great insight into our growth process. The feelings in our body bring ideas into our mind for review and acceptance. If you have shut down your feelings for fear of being hurt, you are not fully capable of living your life.

There is no such thing as a bad feeling. Even if your body is occupied by a deep sadness or injury, the understanding you find by fully experiencing the feeling will bring new insight. When you have understood the meaning behind the feeling, you will be able to accept and release it. God knows there is little value in suffering. It is the understanding and growth that comes through the experience of suffering that has value. You make choices and create your script to further your growth. You must fully experience and feel your story line to grow.

Emotions also come in our physical package. They activate to intensify our response to events in our life. Emotions can help to place a clear and vivid picture in our memory: both in the mind and at a cellular level in our bodies. They are like the fireworks that make the 4th a different experience than any other day in July in the United States.

As we become more aware of the larger picture beyond the Stage, the usefulness of our emotions begins to decline. In contrast, experiencing our feelings without reservation remains essential to fully embracing life. We find the basic vibration of life—LOVE—and its expression—JOY—are not truly emotions. They are beyond the boundaries of the broader physical emotions like anger, frustration, depression, hatred, jealousy, fearfulness, guilt, envy, etc. Even *happiness* is not so much an emotion as our acceptance of WHAT IS, and the gentle appreciation for all things. If all is flowing naturally in our lives, happiness is our natural basic state.

We are always joined with our higher-self. Our Self-incarnate is like a physical connection for this multidimensional Being: the physical can be experienced, and interaction with other actors in physical expression can be conducted. However, the need to have emotionally dramatic and time-consuming reactions to all that happens, becomes less important as the actor becomes more consciously aware of this connection. Instead of the ups and downs most people think of as the normal course of life, a state of centered calmness becomes the norm.

Our reaction to events becomes less severe because there is a sense of objective observation in place. The aware actor views the unfolding scenes as his Play in expression. The value in each experience is the meaning of the symbols understood, and the growth occurring. Riding a roller coaster of emotions does not usually add value.

Emotional swings to extremes can get in the way and extend the time it takes to absorb a lesson. Unchecked worldly emotions can steer us into actions or words that create unnecessary imbalances, or karma, with other actors. Such occurrences will require a resolution that can slow our evolutionary process.

But even as our emotions begin to subside as we take our position as observer, our feelings brought out by the events in our life become ever more pronounced. The feelings in our body act as connections into memories, bringing a deeper knowledge of our Self. We feel the experience, embrace the understanding, release the experience, and move on.

Relationships

Each of us comes into the world alone. We go out alone. While we are here, we savor the experience of our life from our own perspective. The other actors that flow in and out of our script make impressions and create bonds. However it is still only from our own position that we can appreciate our life.

We are champions of our life. Although we serve others through interactions as our Plays coincide, our primary focus must be on our own choices and direction. We are here to devote ourselves to our own life and growth. This is the appropriate area in which we function. Balancing this self-centeredness, with compassion and caring for others, is a challenge. Relationships, therefore, become an art form.

One of the finest feelings, as an adult, is to know oneself as a whole and balanced Being, living consciously, moment-to-moment. Once in this state, we are well prepared to focus our energy on a separate Being, and to have a fulfilling love relationship. A healthy relationship is made up of two such whole individuals. Together, a third energy is formed which emanates the union of love, intentions and creativity of the two individuals combined.

When you have the warm honor of coming across another actor, and have the feeling you have known them before, it is because you have. You will eventually find you have a many-lifetime connection with most people who are central in your script. If you are fortunate enough to have arranged a love relationship or marriage in this life with one of these old friends, you have potential of enjoying a most deep and joyful union. It is a blessing when you can feel a spiritual closeness that goes beyond the boundaries of your own physical body, or even beyond the boundaries of time and space.

To be in a balanced relationship with another actor requires sensitive awareness of this loving process. It asks you to soften your heart at every sense of tension, that you see this other person's divine spiritual self behind their every word and deed, and that you love them as their own unique aspect of God, despite which end of the toothpaste tube they prefer to squeeze first.

No single event in physical existence is worth sweating. What is important is how we continue to choose to interact with other actors on our Stage. Our actions tell everything about how far we have come.

To maintain a supportive, loving relationship is to listen carefully to each other, have compassion for each other, and strive for honest communication. If a misunderstanding exists, clear it up when noticed. Each new moment with one another is best savored if there are no leftover issues from moments past. Clear the small blemishes with heaps of forgiveness and acceptance. Notice them, forgive them, and let them go. Your attentiveness will pay off in a feeling of lightness and affection that makes your individual way even more pleasurable and full.

Once a balanced embrace of two actors is in place, and it is in the highest good for all concerned, another soul can be invited in. A new hero is born into a physical body formed within the loving union of the relationship. So another actor enters into unique, physical expression.

Of course, it is not always in this idyllic condition that new heroes choose to make their entrance onto our Stage. Their parents may not have consciously recognized their choice to have a child. Perhaps the home life is raucous and full of heavy emotions and strong events. These variations simply serve the story line that the actor has come in to experience. None of these individuals needs our sympathy. There is never a reason to feel sorry for someone based on our perception of their life condition. Remember: we each choose our course through life.

Interestingly, the most productive work in a relationship is not found in direct interaction. What brings the greatest benefit is paying close attention to perfecting our **own** expression in every thought, word and deed. It is through growing spiritually oneself, that the depth of quality in our relationships is made greater.

We cannot change another person directly. Usually a lot of time and energy is wasted before we figure this out. The only person over whom we have control, and therefore are equipped to truly change, is ourself.

Remember, as we are in a relationship here on Earth, our higher-selves are also in communication regarding the evolving relationship. As one individual evolves and becomes more enLIGHTened, the Universal law of Like Energies takes effect. The partner will either choose to follow the other actor's example and move to a higher vibration, or the gap will become too great, and he will choose to leave. **Fearing change in a relationship has caused many an actor to falter in their own expansion of Self.**

We serve as mirrors for one another in all of our relationships. Since like energy attracts and abides with like energy, it is not difficult to see how this can be true. When you see anger, frustration or fear in your partner's expression, look to your own inner condition for some unnoticed behavior that fits the same energy pattern. Negative energy cannot support itself for long unless other actors feed it by giving it attention. Find and resolve the negative energy within yourself, ignore the negative energy in your partner, and the dis-ease in the relationship will be healed without one word spoken.

Never forget: one of the best ways to dispel a negative situation is with a heartfelt laugh. It is a fast and foolproof barometer of how well you are on track. If you are not laughing as you journey, then not only your relationships, but also your personal existence is out-of-balance and lacking spontaneity. Find what makes you smile, and make it a constant ingredient in your life.

The New Millennium

The underlying truth is that we are all One. Despite the illusion of physical separateness, our souls connect through the soles of our feet resting on Mother Earth. Our connections from inside—at the heart—bind us into one common mind. Our energies join with that of the Earth, to form the total quality of energy on our planet.

Humanity has a consciousness. This consciousness has been far below perceivable levels in the past, but the voice of our combined consciousness is rising. The day will come when we will feel and hear silently in our minds this common voice of brotherhood. Our separate paths are carving a new dimension into our future together.

This is an exciting time on our planet. You have chosen to be here at the most fascinating crossroads in recorded history. Call it what you will: the Age of Aquarius, the New Age, the

Golden Age. What we will create together, will be a truly new
way for Humanity to exist on our planet. In every moment,
our combined choices are creating the dynamic events that are
building our tomorrow.

Many sources are bringing forth information about the
changes ahead. Our perceived separateness will pass, and our
true Oneness will regain its place of honor in our conscious
minds. Angels will walk among us, and God's Love will be
common knowledge. Heaven will again be evident upon the
Earth.

We are here to work with our beautiful planet. To care for
her and each other as we hone our personal attributes in physical expression. Our planet is going through changes that will
alter her landmasses. She must purge the poisons with which
we have plagued her. She must follow her own natural path
toward the purest expression of her true nature.

For those who choose to leave during these dramatic years
of change, there will be a myriad of exciting natural events to
savor as their personal curtain comes down. For those of us
who choose to stay, life will require we unite in a new form of
cooperation. Our old ways will be left behind, as we create a
new way of being.

The dramatic changes that will mark a course towards a new
way of life on Earth are already started. We sometimes forget
how magnificently adaptive we humans are. We can absorb
great personal change in our life, and simply do what needs to
be done to continue on. With trust in God's Plan, and an ear
to our inner guidance, there is no need for fear. In fact, fear is
one thing that has no place in our New World based in Love.

Even the earth changes that will take place are being dynamically rewritten. As more individuals choose love, the scenarios become less severe, responding to the heightened awareness and vibration.

There are very different soul ages among actors in expression on Earth today. Some souls have been here many times and are nearing the end of the cycle of physical incarnations. Others are fairly new at it, and feel quite confused by the complexities of life here. Most actors are somewhere in-between. Personal reaction to what is unfolding on our planet will vary accordingly.

Humanity is dividing into two camps. One group of humanity will come into a condition of conscious awareness of their thoughts, words and actions. By taking conscious responsibility for its combined scripts, and seeking expression of its true Self-essence, this group will raise the vibration on the planet to a new level. The second group will choose to depart, rather than remain on a planet that no longer provides the quality of energy required for its script.

Each individual will ultimately be in one or the other group, propelled by their choices made in each moment as they live their life. Many individuals actively seek to know their personal relationship with God. They seek answers, strive to move these Loving concepts into their hearts, and finally into natural expression in their lives. These souls lead the way toward a higher planetary vibration. Following closely are simple unassuming people who naturally choose gentle, loving behavior. They show care and compassion for everyone they meet. These pure children of God improve the quality of our Life by their presence. The second group will be made up of those individuals choosing to remain unchanged in their approach to life, even as the vibration on our planet increases. Whatever each individual decides for themselves, the Universe will lovingly support their desires.

The tension and craziness of our current times will crescendo as the difference increases between those choosing to remain and those moving unconsciously toward exit. We will be witnessing a natural process that will expose the heightened difference in vibratory levels of these two groups of souls. As actors who cling to their old, lower vibration ways leave our Stage through illness, "accidents" or natural disaster, the average vibration of Humanity will begin to soar. This will serve to make those who remain immersed in the old ways feel even more exposed and angry.

But at one moment in time, the transition will be complete. Our one consciousness will emerge into our waking minds, and we will all KNOW our combined truth. With the vibration of our planet and souls so enhanced, we will all become aware of what has previously been hidden behind the Veil. Our time of loving cooperation—of Heaven on Earth—will grace our planet.

This is the promise of much information coming into our planet, as well as seen in those very old documents and books, such as the Bible. The exact way in which it comes to pass will be dynamically created by our planet and peoples combined, as we move through each moment of each day.

We all influence the Whole. Although a high level outline of our planet's script has been penned, the dynamic expression during the unfolding will create the details. What will flow into being on the other side of this transition will be a much simpler life enjoyed by fewer Human Beings. We will find ourselves joined by Beings of other species from other worlds to form a balanced oasis in space.

Death

We have spoken of our production meetings before birth, and our dynamic scripts in physical expression, but how does it end? When is it time for the curtain to come down on our Play?

The timing and choice of the circumstances remain in our hero's hands. We constantly have conferences with our higher-self, usually on an unconscious level. When the time comes that either all the valuable juice of experience has been squeezed from our script, or we agree we are ill fitted to gain any additional experience of value from our current position, an agreement is struck to close the Play. At this point the script's purpose shifts to constructing the events needed to attain the selected exit. A plane that crashes without survivors is filled with individual souls who have chosen this point to depart.

Death is a very personal happening in the actor's script. The level at which each is consciously aware of this agreement differs widely. It is felt in as many different ways as there are participants.

Our modern medical science, with its focus on keeping everyone alive as its highest ideal, can interfere more than help. If appropriate to the script, living wills provide a legal way to ensure the least interference when the chosen time to go Home has arrived. However, the course created may well include a dramatic scenario of battling an illness that plays out over many months, ending in death. Even in such a situation, there has been value in the time for all those who were involved. The very real grief felt at such times of loss makes "value" a strange word to use. But, looking back later, it is recognized that such intense times of **living** every moment, condense the time needed to further one's personal growth.

For most people, death is cloaked in fear. It represents the gravest, fastest change from the known to the unknown available in physical expression. Many find throughout their lives that change brings with it insecurities and uncomfortable situations.

But let me assure you, what waits on the far side of the Veil is a far grander place than could ever exist in our coarse, three-dimensional world. As this extreme change of death bursts into our consciousness, we encounter the most familiar and supportive environment we could possibly have imagined as an actor. Our Being becomes flooded with full exposure to the unconditional Love that flows through the heart of all Creation. We reunite with our higher-self, rejoin the forgotten Whole and cannot even remember what fear felt like. Many personal accounts with near-death experiences are becoming better known. These accounts describe their sense of "*going Home.*"

There is no gate on Heaven through which one must negotiate safe passage. No need for reentrance exists, since it was only illusion that you were ever separated from your Source. There is only complete openness, total acceptance, unconditional Love, and Peace without end. You will encounter no Hell, unless from

strong beliefs while in Play, you choose to create this hereafter
for yourself.

There are no imposed rules that govern such things.
Your essence is entering the domain of unconditional Love
and infinite patience. You can create for yourself whatever you
choose to find after death. Then, when you tire of your limited
creation, your choice will shift to allowing all that can be. The
glorious and beautiful simplicity of being will open your eyes
to your soul group and friends.

Once passed from physical existence to the afterworld,
your creative prowess comes into full use. You move effortlessly.
All doubts and concerns dissolve: their coarse nature cannot
exist once you are flooded with this pure White Light of Love.
Your Being will know itself completely, without shame, no
secrets to cast shadows. The soul essences of all friends and
others in your soul group become available for interaction and
joyous reunions. Since you are of a unique vibration, you will
attract and be with others of similar or harmonic vibration.

One choice tidbit to expect after death is this: *all Beings with
whom you have a relationship will be available to you.* Even those
still in physical expression as actors have a higher-self you can
hug and enjoy! You will experience no barriers, no limitations,
once you choose to fully awaken after your transition from the
physical.

There is no Judgment Day filled with guilt and regrets. We
come into the physical world as divine spiritual Beings, seeking
experience and growth. And as this whole and divine Being,
we review the lessons learned and the happenings experienced
within our own completed Play. An objective assessment

emerges, brimming with love and understanding. This broadened experience of oneself is fully integrated, and is retained in our essence as if another ring in our tree's trunk. All that has gone before, and the potentials yet to be explored, are savored while we devise our next adventure in the physical.

You are a unique expression of the infinite creative force of God. Your consciousness never dies. You simply go through transitions as you move through lives. You are not only loved unconditionally, but you are in truth made of the purest form of Love vibration. The physical Creation we observe, along with an infinite array of other levels and galaxies we can only imagine, are all sustained within the complex yet simple web of Love that is God.

In the same moment, we are a simple human standing in a grocery line, as well as one unique tone in the infinite symphony that is the entirety of Creation itself. We are never really alone; we can only choose to hold the perception of being alone. No one is unimportant. Everyone has impact on everyone and everything else. Every choice each of us makes in every moment affects the shape and texture of the tapestry of Existence.

Why Am I Here?

IF YOU HAVE NOT SET THIS BOOK DOWN and walked easily away, we can be quite sure you are one of those humans who has chosen to stay on Earth rather than seek an early departure. While here, you will find a rich body of experiences to foster your growth. You have come to our beautiful planet at this time so your essence can lend support during the magnificent metamorphosis that is occurring.

If you begin to feel truth in this idea, do not panic! There is nothing you must suddenly change about your life to prepare for your responsible position. The exact way in which you participate will flow naturally as the script of your life unfolds, moment-by-moment.

Unless you feel a strong heartfelt impulse to do something, take no special action. All you need do is follow your instincts, and remain consciously aware of your thoughts, words and deeds. *Leading your life in accord with its natural flow, is what you have come here to do.*

Few among us will accomplish anything so dramatic that our fellow actors will know us by name around the planet. But by being true to yourself and your inner guidance, you will help others to move through this transitional period with grace. Others learn from your example in the simple daily things that come naturally to you.

Realize your spiritual base in every moment. Know what you view is your Play. Appreciate and give thanks for the dynamics in your script that you have created for yourself. Appreciate and thank those actors in interaction with you, and the Beings from beyond for their kind assistance. They provide the fertile soil for your growth, so the seeds of your greatest potential may bud forth.

For further details of a personal nature, turn inward. Spend quiet time strengthening your connection with your higher-self, guides and Spirit. Watch your unfolding life for hints and messages gently camouflaged in your daily activities. Accept those changes that come to you as willingly as they are offered. It is by stepping confidently through the doors of opportunity that come into view that your life evolves.

In July 1996, I took a week long vacation to Washington state to visit family and close friends. As I spent quality time in each household, I felt its distinct life rhythm. Along with feeling and appreciating the differences of each, I became aware of something about myself. It felt as if my life rhythm was coming to a standstill!

At first I felt quite frightened that the sense of direction in which my life moved, could be approaching such a neutral condition. Upon arriving home to Florida, I felt without direction and a bit depressed. I had to sit quietly and wonder what Divine Oneness was sharing with me. I had several dreams that pointed out the mismatch between my true nature and my work world at the time, which was full-time employment in a corporate office, filled with the tensions and pressures of the tenuous times.

Finally, I realized what was happening. I was on the verge of making a dramatic shift in my life. An act in my Play was coming to completion, and a far different and more exciting act would be dawning. To provide myself with the appropriate dramatic flare, I knew it was important to become still, so that the new direction could start crisply, without misplaced momentum to overcome.

My mind's patterned urge to muster some action, any action, just for the sake of motion, was brought under control; I allowed the process to take over. Blind faith can feel disturbing when no action is the appropriate action.

When you question why you are here, the best place to find your answer is inside yourself. Your life reflects your script, your day in the Sun. "Yeah, yeah," you say, "I've heard this before. Yet no matter where I look, I cannot find the story board in there to give me the clues I seek!" Well, look around you then. Look back over the years of your life. Are there seemingly unrelated experiences that in hindsight, begin to develop a pattern that makes you think of a certain flavor? Do you recognize patterns in your life that you wish could be broken, making room for you to move into uncharted waters?

Your life is just that, *your life*. It is a dynamic creation of which you are in charge. The theme(s) that run through it are hints to help you perfect the focus of your energy. You are here to find those things that make your heart sing. Once immersed in these activities, you find personal satisfaction beyond your grandest dreams.

The following are samples of information that can provide hints about what you have come here to do: where you were born; the parents you chose; the financial condition into which you were born; the schools you attended; friends and natural abilities that have caught your attention. No one else can make it clear for you. There are others of whom you can choose to ask questions. But remember, it was your decision to ask a particular friend, psychic, psychologist, etc. If you earnestly seek clues about yourself, your answers will come: perhaps through the filtered words of these other people, or through the body sensations within yourself during meditation. Your answers will be found.

If you begin to suspect a certain skill or ability as the thing you chose to develop in this lifetime, test it by spending more of your time in the practice of whatever it is. If spending your time in this way makes you feel happy—if hours slip away in the space of a few moments—you are probably onto the right track. However, if things start getting complicated or difficult, it may either not yet be the right time, or perhaps it is simply a dead end. You will know. You are the only one who will *know*.

Once you begin to focus your time and energy into the practice of your natural abilities, you will find there are people who are in need of your skills. The act of practicing will seemingly create the demand. You will find yourself in the right place at the right time, ready willing and able to fulfill the needs of your clientele.

Conversely, if you think you are doing just the right thing, and there is no one in need of your service, then a recheck with your heart is in order. Either you are in the wrong place (pack the U-Haul), or you misread some of your clues and you are off track. Perhaps an element is missing in what you are doing; or some personal lesson must be recognized and accepted to clear the way.

So what if you do not know what you want to be when you grow up? Simply behave in each moment the way you feel is right for you, and all will fall into place when the time comes. Besides, you can always choose to re-decide what you want to be, or even whether you want to grow up at all. Your right to change your mind and re-decide never goes away.

Most actors do not easily accept that we each create our own world. Each major change we make in our life—perhaps a physical move to another state—starts from a seed thought to blossom forth into an event. It begins within our heart, planted under the watchful guardianship of our wonderful mind. If the idea has value for us, and fits the natural flow of our life, it will grow.

One day you see a travel bureau poster depicting sunny Florida. Perhaps you decide to visit on vacation. When there, you feel at peace, as if you were *home*. Back home, you begin to pick up newspapers from areas in Florida that attract you. One day this newspaper's classified section is advertising a job that fits you perfectly. You respond, you interview, and you are hired. You release your old location and move into a totally unknown situation, because you know it is right for you (your heart has smiled at you the whole way).

This may seem like small coincidences that compounded to deliver you to a new mailing address, but the process is not haphazard. If Florida had not been your next destination, this chain of events would not have happened. You would not have noticed what was in the travel bureau window. You would have continued vacationing at your timeshare in the Smoky Mountains. You would never have picked up an out-of-state newspaper. Something—everything—would have discouraged this decision.

You are here as a physical expression of your higher, spiritual self. Whether you are consciously aware of it or not, communications between the two of you occur. You are helped, nudged, guided into choices that serve your higher purpose: your life's purpose. Even when not fully aware of your course in this life, or the reasons underlying this incarnation, you are always shepherded gently in directions that will serve you best. You are far from alone as you sashay through life. However, the final decisions, whether to follow these inclinations and take advantage of the life opportunities offered, is always yours alone. Free will remains your greatest gift.

Now maybe all of this sounds a bit too simplistic. Maybe what I have experienced in my relatively sweet and easy life is a far cry from where you find yourself. Maybe you feel stuck in an inner city somewhere. Your mother is a drug addict, and you do not know who your father was. Life seems too dark and difficult to be changed. And as far as my trying to hang the responsibility of where you find yourself on you, you'd be damned if you would ever have created such a Hellhole for yourself!

Well, I don't care if you are chained to a wall in a third-world prison, left to rot. You have yourself, and you have an unalienable right to live your life in accord with your true nature. Even if someone coerces you into saying or doing something you would not freely say or do, they have not won, nor have you lost. If you make it your highest duty to listen and make contact with the inner you—to get to know this Being—then remain true to your basic nature, you will have let your Light shine. Even if you die chained to that wall, never seeing the sky again, you worked within your life conditions, and with conscious awareness lived each of your moments while alive.

Even if your physical body is confined, allowing far less movement than you would like, your heart and mind are always free to soar. No one, other than you, can confine them.

I have read of monks in Tibet who choose to have themselves sealed in caves, where they would sit and meditate. Helpers would agree to serve them while entombed. They required little food, because they were not really functioning in their physical body. Instead they allowed their consciousness to move free of their bodies, to travel the Earth and other worlds. They learned to transcend their physical limitation, and travel freely wherever their consciousness roamed.

If you look around you and say your life "sucks," then *do something about it!* Recognize your power to create new situations in your life. Begin to decide what you want to change. You must take each step after tiny step, while moving towards what you want.

Make a pact with yourself to introduce one new thing each day that nurtures you. Go to the library and search out a short poem that warms your heart. Go to a new place—a park, a restaurant, etc.—feel and enjoy its unique ambiance. Find someone willing to massage your neck and shoulders for three minutes. Seek out whatever brings you a few moments of pleasure.

These adventures loosen the structure of your current life. They introduce fresh air, and awaken the understanding that things can change. You can give yourself a better life. Only you can figure out what aspects in your life you want changed.

Gather yourself together in a quiet place. Yes, you can find one if you are sincere. Then ask yourself what life you would be living if there were **no limitations.**

Look within. Search for your heart's desires, and visualize what it would be like. Focus on this vision and make it real. See it move. Smell any fragrances in your envisioned scene. Feel the temperature on your skin. Listen for the sounds around you. Touch the surface of an object near you. *Be there. Make it real. MAKE IT WHAT YOU WANT…* You, my friend, have just placed an order with the Universe.

Visit this image often. Know that this is where you are meant to be. Feel yourself being there. Only share your experience with friends who will support you in your desire to change your life. Avoid those who will feel envious, negative or laugh at your strange ideas. Nurture this dream as you would a delicate plant entrusted to your care. Feed it your attention, and embrace it with love.

If you are dissatisfied with where you are in your life, you must detach your attention from your current conditions before you can see where you want to be. You may have difficulties doing this. It may be hard for you to see past your current life, to what you would truly want for yourself. You may be so full of anger over "why me," or what others are "doing" to you, that your attention is not available to look beyond it. If this is true of your situation, you must release these things from your Being before you can focus. You are in need of a healing.

Anger is a powerful dampener of your natural energy flow. It causes you to clamp down and freeze-frame on a specific event, person or thing as the source of your pain. Everything you do serves as little more than a diversion before you come back to this unquenchable sense of anger.

If you are someone who has difficulty experiencing your anger directly, you may turn it inwards creating a dark depression for yourself. If a deep sadness fills your heart, you will likely have to first discover the anger of which it is made, before you can identify the ultimate source of your distress.

If you do not know what you are angry at, watch your reaction to situations that come up in your life. Ask your guides that the cause of your distress be made clear. If you are a seeker of this knowledge, it will be shown to you in your life events. Look at those times when you overreact to a situation. Here will be the clues to solve this mystery.

Once you understand the source of your anger, there are many paths to releasing it from your life. You may seek a counselor who can offer advice and techniques for working through it. You may spend time before a mirror, talking to this anger-provoking person or situation, to vent this pent-up energy. You may roll up a towel and beat on your bed until the anger rolls out and subsides. But, the healing event that ultimately releases its hold on your Being permanently, is to **forgive.**

Catherine Ponder has written several books on the subject of forgiveness. She points out that *Forgiveness gives something positive for something negative.* The Act of forgiving changes the anger into something no longer rooted in you. It dissolves the anger, and it is gone.

Start showing your anger the door as soon as you recognize it as one of the elements blocking your energy from flowing freely in your body and your life. If you feel stuck, and cannot see beyond what today is made of, then you are quite safe in assuming you are harboring anger.

You cannot just bury anger to be free. It will fester and grow more virulent while living in your subconscious. You cannot reason with anger. If your anger is with a particular person, it may not even be possible for you to come to a common resolution with them.

Releasing your anger and hurt is not about anyone else. It is about **you.** Your responsibility, your sphere of influence, is with yourself. You can release your anger, and heal yourself, by forgiving.

> *I forgive myself. I forgive everyone, everything, every memory, and every experience in need of forgiveness, from the past and present. I forgive all of these things NOW!*

These are only words. You may not even mean them when you say them. But your heart hears these words. Your body absorbs the vibrations of these words. Your higher-self and guides hear what you say and honor your desire in those areas where they can be of assistance. When these (or your own similar) words are repeated hourly, daily, weekly, whenever seems appropriate, a cleansing is set into motion that will serve you well.

If you know yourself to hold anger, and do not feel this technique is meant for you, then I would ask if you are really willing to be free from your restriction? Is there a reason you do not feel you deserve peace of mind? Is your ego controlling your decision, saying, "These strong feelings show you are alive. If you desert them, there will be nothing left of you." (Do not listen to your ego. It fears the loss of its power, and has no interest in your well being.) Ask yourself why you are unwilling to make a positive move in search of releasing these negative blockages. Do you have an answer?

The following visualization was shared with me long ago. When I first did it, the results amazed me. It very accurately shows how you truly feel about yourself.

> *Sit quietly and close your eyes. In your mind's eye, see yourself comfortably seated in a chair with another chair facing you approximately four feet away. Then imagine the person whom you love most (living or dead) seated in this other chair facing you. Feel your love for them. Look into their eyes and enjoy their company. When you have fully appreciated them and experienced your deep love for them,* **change the person sitting across from you to be yourself.** *Do your feelings about this "other person" change? How do your feelings change?*

When I first did this exercise, I was surprised that I could not afford myself the same level of love and appreciation as I gave my loved one. Here we are, truly alone with ourselves on this planet. Yes, other actors flow in and out of our life. Maybe some even come in and stay for a prolonged period, bringing us great joy. However, the only person we can be absolutely sure will always be around is our Self.

If you cannot love, appreciate and nurture yourself, you are not well equipped to love, appreciate or nurture others. Using statements of your desires to release anger and hurt, to reclaim this blocked energy for positive joyful use in your life, is a most deeply nurturing act. Of all Beings on this planet, you are most deserving of this gift. Only you can provide it for yourself.

Be honest with yourself as you observe your behavior. If you catch yourself playing the reciprocal game of resentment, assigning blame to inflict guilt upon others, or wearing the heavy cloak of martyrdom, recognize what you are doing. These are all smoke screens, designed by your ego to pull your attention away from your real purpose here. You must be willing to leave these small negative behaviors behind. You must be consciously on guard for their appearance, and drop them from your actions like hot potatoes when discovered.

If you are in a negative discussion with someone, turn and walk away. If you are critical of your own choices and achievements, forgive yourself. Allow yourself to accept the lessons learned, and move on without further focus on this past. When you recall bits and pieces from your earlier life that bring pain with them, embrace them for the life experience they provided, forgive the experience, and turn your attention away.

You have a mission—even if it seems like *Mission Impossible*—you are here for a reason. Discovering this reason, and allowing your life to be gently shaped to support this design, is where your energies are meant to be focused. It happens little by little in your every thought, word and deed. In the simplest things you do.

You move though life metaphorically in harness, hitched to your wagon cradling your purpose in life. If you feel pressure on your shoulders from pulling forward into your harness, then you are moving too fast. It should feel like a mantle of beautiful clothes resting gently on your shoulders. Forcing forward sets up an energy scenario of forcefulness, and you find yourself in a battle of wills with everything and everyone. Pressing too quickly will feel like a major resistance to your progress. Relax into the natural flow of yourself and life becomes fluid.

The frame of mind with which you move forward in each moment, creates the chord that will color the experiences you have. In every respect, you create the fullness of your own experiences. When the heart guides your direction, your script writes itself. Everything becomes natural and fluid. You cannot help but be in the right place at the right time, to meet your fondest dreams coming into being.

Every Answer Is In Your Heart

OUR MINDS ARE A MIRACULOUS MAZE of electromagnetic activity. They can draw together diverse ideas into a new concept, far more dazzling than its parts. Our mind perceives our life, and continually organizes ideas into logical pictures. This gives us the clearinghouse needed to expose issues on which it is appropriate to be making decisions. However, our mind can become our own worst enemy if our heart does not oversee its activity.

The heart provides a synthesizing energy. It brings the physical aspects in which we live, together with spiritual aspects that flow into us from the Universe. It is literally the coming together of the physical and spiritual within us.

The heart uses tender compassionate wisdom to bridge this gap between physical experiences and spiritual knowing. The heart negotiates the permission for us to experience all aspects of ourselves. This *open* condition allows our intuition and gentle suggestive urges to come to our notice. It is here, in the heart, that we become physically aware of the sensations of information coming into us from our higher-self, guides and Spirit.

It is the mind's place to take direction from our more subtle, feeling heart. The mind can then hold the seed idea as if a rough sketch on a canvas, thoughtfully pulling together other thoughts and information bits to foster the idea's growth.

When you decide what to do next by looking at how you might control or manipulate things into going your way, you are bypassing your natural creative ability. Without your heart's involvement, the idea is cold and forced.

When ideas come into your mind, stop and feel your body. Ask yourself if the idea is a creation of your mind alone, or does your heart warm with the thought? With your heart supporting and encouraging an idea, it is born in love on a sure course to fulfillment.

As an actor in Play on Earth, you are a unique Being, responsible for your thoughts, words and deeds. As you open to the more subtle flow in your life, you will find less interest in getting worked up over an idea.

The old you might latch onto a thought and begin turning it this way and that, analyzing it and running it through what-if scenarios. Then, selecting the scenario most advantageous, you might begin searching for things you could do or say to certain people to grease the way. Finally you arrive at this "Plan," and roll it into motion. But your carefully chosen word to this person does not make them do what you expect. And if that part of the plan falters, what else will need to be reengineered to regain your projected end result?

While in the heat of your mental reverie, you have forgotten to live your life. The events that happened while you were focused in your mind, constructing your plan, are done and gone. You did not notice; you were too busy in your head. This is not how life is designed to work. All you can ever know for sure is your own perception of what is happening in this moment: the eternal NOW. Time churning in your mind might be fun, but do not mistake this recreation for actual living.

Life happens in each moment. It is dynamic, creative, exciting—it is real. You say something. Someone responds with words. If you are in balance and centered, you are experiencing the entire exchange down to a cellular level. What comes out of your exchange is a joint creation of both actors' energies. It is not made of what-if scenarios. Life is made up of *what is*.

When we appreciate the simple interactions with people and places in our life, each thing naturally leads to another. From a relaxed position, we respond to what is happening from our heart. We *feel* what is going on. Our mind takes on a subservient rather than a dominant role. It helps us notice similarities and differences in those things around us. It assists in seeking and finding the clues cloaked in symbols abundantly flowing in our life.

During the daily process of living your life, ideas revolving around long range preferences come up in your mind. If these directions have arrived in full accord of your heart's wishes, they begin to simmer on a back burner of your mind. If the young idea matches your life's direction, it will stay with you. You will begin to notice reference to it in written material you find, or it will come up in conversation. If this begins to happen, you can be assured the idea is well founded.

The idea will remain with you in a simple form, without any more detail than your moment-by-moment living has provided.

Then one day, when your life events have brought you to the appropriate time in your script, you will see before you the full expression of that simple thought. It may not be precisely the color or size of your first thought, but it will be the natural product, dynamically created by your life from the seed planted earlier.

The heart serves as a loving conduit for an infinite variety of seed thoughts. Whether from your own internal timing, or from a gentle prodding received from your higher-self or guides, ideas flowing into your mind from the heart will serve you far better than your mind running off with the bit clenched between its teeth.

Be kind and patient with your wonderful mind. Watch its activity with the wisdom of your heart. Laugh kindly when you find it getting far too excited or serious over some inconsequential thing. Your mind has probably lived many years in control of the decision process. Its holographic projection of you—the ego—will not step down from power voluntarily. You will need to lovingly curtail its antics.

As you consciously watch the source of your living process, as it is created from within, you will begin to see that ideas coming through the heart yield a higher quality outcome. Those ideas forced into existence from the ego usually meet greater resistance in execution, and provide no natural momentum into your next life vignette.

When you catch yourself operating in the old way, just stop, forgive yourself and take some deep breaths. Ask your heart for the appropriate next step, and lead your mind gently into recognizing and accepting its wisdom.

Moving too fast is a sure way to overrun your next natural step. It will trip you up and disrupt the flow. If you are moving too slowly for others' taste, it is definitely *their* problem (in perception), not yours. If you are moving too slowly for **yourself,** then your perception needs some adjustment. Your ego has sneaked back for another run at control, or you have forgotten to be patient with the process and accepting of what occurs.

Life perceived through the heart is very simple, and contains many recurring refrains. On the other hand, if your life seems complex and difficult, your ego-mind is leading the way. It has bamboozled you into a corner, where you timidly watch with amazement at all the intricate things with which it has filled and overfilled your days. Your body is racked with tension, and you feel powerless to take control for fear all will fall into pieces.

Well, take heart. It may be exactly what is needed for your physically oriented world to come tumbling down. What is the worst thing that would happen if you stepped off your synthetic merry-go-round?

If you are living from a superficially constructed position, your life may well need *leveling* before you can gain balance. If your life is full of artificial things and actions, the energy you create and experience is far different from the Divine vibration of natural forms. Such unnatural constructions require a great deal of energy and attention to maintain them. The lack of efficiency can keep you on the edge of exhaustion. Would loosing control of this difficult complexity really be that bad? A more natural path rising from the ashes may be just what you yearn for.

You can take back your life. Start with the first thing you notice that your heart is not behind. Did guilt cause you to make a commitment to do something that does not fit you? Bow out. Remember how to say "No." Do not be concerned about letting anyone down. Our plays within plays are all dynamic. If you say No, there will be someone there to fulfill the task (if it was indeed needed at all).

The finest act you can perform for every living creature upon our planet, is to focus your energy on what is important to you, from the heart. Do nothing that seems empty or hollow. Even if this means you sit home alone for the next month, take the opportunity to get in touch with yourself. The real you is the one who flows naturally into being through the heart.

Impulses coming through your heart seem to have a life of their own. You will feel passion in your Being. You will feel alive. You will BE ALIVE, possibly for the first time!

F I V E

Everything Is Made Of Energy; Everything Is Connected

ALL OF OUR KNOWN EXISTENCE is made up of microscopic particles vibrating at various frequencies, interacting with each other in various ways. How we perceive the scene is usually much different.

So Much The Same

As infants, we do not differentiate between objects. Having just arrived from the Oneness of the afterworld, where all is known instinctively within a quiet calmness, the brash physical world appears confusing. The dynamics of the physical world are far outside the young one's experience. A new way of grasping what is occurring must be found. So starts our actor's indoctrination into the physical world, as his caretakers share their understanding. The boundaries separating things begin to be drawn, and the young one learns what is expected of him.

It is difficult to look around ourselves and see anything other than what we have been conditioned to perceive. Every object we identify with a separate word is in truth a loosely organized system of molecules, riddled with huge spaces between the vibrating fragments. Our language and well-intentioned instruction, have suspended our ability to see beyond the obvious to the real structure of physical matter. There is nothing in our everyday lives that require this more accurate understanding.

I had been intrigued while listening to an audiotape titled, *Seven Spiritual Laws of Success*, recorded by Deepak Chopra. He spoke about perceptions of our physical world based on quantum physics. From this perspective, he explained how boundaries between things and people become far less discernible. However, I was a bit disappointed when I went to the public library to do some research. I had hoped to glimpse a further expression of this hazy netherworld I sensed in the words of Dr. Chopra. Instead, many pages presented precise documentation about this microscopic world, dealing with the structure and behavior of the atom and its associated atomic particles.

My disappointment was not so much with the information itself, but from the fact that these scientific writings had not once shifted from the microscope view to discuss the meaning of these discoveries on our more immediate human level, as Dr. Chopra had done. I had to be satisfied with personally assuming that the similarity in behavior in all atoms applies to the broader scope of energy interactions in our everyday world.

Our unseen physical world that can be verified by science, operates on identical atomic structures. Whether observing a boulder in a canyon or a world-class runner, these microscopic characteristics operate identically. It is the consciousness that inhabits the physical material that gives it a form we identify as a separate thing or Being.

When you are crossing a bridge in your automobile, you are looking upon water, land and air. You can sit idly in your mind, accepting the surface impressions of the elements before you, or you can look deeper into what is presented. Beneath the surface of that water swim all kinds of fish and mammals, like dolphins and whales; crustaceans, kelp and microscopic creatures swirl in the currents. To the skies there are birds of every description: ducks, geese, sea gulls, herons and cranes, hawks, eagles, wrens and robins. On the land climb and slither a lush assortment of creatures, some more visible then others; the trees and grasses, flowers and scrubs adorn the landscape as far as our eye can imagine.

All of these things, and much more beyond, live and die in the sphere of our experience. We cannot know each personally, but they are interwoven into the very same system of life upon our beautiful planet as we are. If you would like to have a deeper experience of your connection with all life forms, allow yourself to feel their presence. Reach your senses out to meet them.

As you watch a sea bird alter his flight and suddenly dip low to snag an edible bite, feel your own muscles matching his effort as he is driven to satisfy his hunger. Feel the bird's excitement and anticipation as strong wings move him into position. See the water looming up quickly as last moment adjustments bring success or failure. Soar with him again as the tasty bit is grasped and tossed expertly down the gullet. You are not the bird, but he is a part of you. Allow your imagination to share his experience.

Everything you perceive as a part of your physical world, is made up of the same materials as yourself. Each creature's conscious energy forms and maintains its physical shape while it is alive. All these unique energies interact with one another. The energy gently pulls like energy, and pushes dissimilar energy, creating the continually changing arena.

Even with all of this dynamic change, everything, in every moment, is always in perfect balance. As personal choices are made, movement in the energy causes all things to shift accordingly, to maintain this perfect balance.

Time

An element in our life that helps hide the true united nature of Existence is our clock. While in physical form, we experience time as sequential events. Not much we can change here. It is simply an attribute of our physical world. However, we strap watches to our wrists, and hang clocks on many walls, so we can count the seconds that separate the past from our future.

Knowing what time it is (now) can be useful. Using time allows people to coordinate their plan to show up at restaurants and sporting events at the same time. Agree upon a place and a time, and any number of individuals can consciously come together for a mutual purpose. We have calendars to help us extend the scope of our predetermined meeting. However, all this is but agreed upon measurements so we can participate in coordinated activities. Time and dates themselves mean nothing. Life is lived in the perpetual NOW.

When you close your eyes, do you feel the throb of the seconds passing by? If you are a Westerner, holding down a

nine-to-five job, it is quite likely that you do. I felt the illusion of
time's movement—once—some *time* ago. Our mental journeys
to relive and reexamine events from the past, and our excursions
into imagining our future, all conspire to maintain our sense of
a movement of time. They lock our belief into this stream of
time passing at a rapid speed.

Today (at this moment) I feel no passage of time. I recognize
yesterday was Tuesday and tomorrow will be Thursday, but
the clock on my wrist only reads what time it is *now*. Even the
sweep of the second hand is only possible as I agree to believe
my memory concerning its previous position.

As you become more focused on what is happening in each
moment, as it happens, you will also hear and feel the tick-tick-
tick become silent. The sense of sand through the hourglass
will end. It is a gloriously peaceful place!

Once you have come to live in the moment, you will begin to
experience the fluid quality of time. Although the clock on the
wall will say thirty minutes have passed, you will have experienced the sense of an hour or more, or perhaps much less than
a typical thirty minutes. Although you will agree to honor the
clock's information, you will find your life's needs will shape
your sense about the amount of time you have at your disposal.

To test your time sense, close your eyes while you wait in
your car for a traffic light to change. If you are familiar with
the route, you probably have a good idea of how long it will be
before the light changes. Keep your eyes closed until you think
it is about time. Then open your eyes and look at the light.
I will bet the first time you do this you will not have kept your
eyes closed long enough. With your eyes open and all the things

to grab your attention, the time will seem shorter than with your eyes closed. Even though the time frames are perceived differently, you can be assured an equal number of seconds has elapsed.

Have you ever experienced an automobile or similar accident? In a typical experience, the seconds pass more like minutes. The action appears as if in slow motion, as one's total awareness focuses intensely in the NOW. In this example, time elongates, while every detail is tattooed upon one's mind. It does not take much experimentation to realize that time is much more fluid and elastic than our clocks let on.

If you are feeling anxious, allow yourself to close your eyes and take a short break. Closing your eyes is the same as closing out chaos, while abiding with your quiet, natural self. Even the two and three minutes' pause at traffic lights can help you regain your composure and balance. The restorative quality available to you in a period of time has little to do with the quantity of the seconds.

Once having said this, I must share with you a shift that is occurring in our physical world's clock. Einstein suggested that as an object approaches the speed of light, its shape becomes distorted. In a similar way, our time measurement is being distorted. Our planet is changing. The frequency of our world is increasing. As our physical world's vibration rises, the structure on which our clocks measure our seconds is being compressed.

I doubt there is anyone among us who does not feel that they have less time today than they did several years ago. Although we like to assign blame, saying our lives are more full of responsibilities and interests today than when we were young, this increase in activity accounts for only a small proportion of the change in our general time sense.

Time IS moving faster! Although it has been slowly quickening over the last 2,000 years, it is beginning to speed up at a greater rate. We will find over the next ten to fifteen years that we will be forced to simplify our lives, because *there will not be enough time to live the complicated lives we lead now!*

If you do not believe this, test it for yourself. Take an afternoon, or the next day you have no specific plans or commitments, and stay at home. Do not watch TV, listen to the radio, or check the clock. Do not wash clothes or run the dishwasher. Do nothing that measures out a segment of time. Instead, read, relax, do some chores around the house, play solitaire, or whatever strikes your fancy. Just be. If, as the sun begins to set, you do not feel as if it has passed in a heart's beat, I will be amazed.

Increasing Frequencies

Our entire world is changing. As the frequencies with which our planet and environment resonate increases, organizations and forms of the older, coarser vibration will begin to falter and change. Over the past several years, we have seen amazing shifts in our political and national structures. Communism fell, and the USSR came apart at the seams. The Berlin Wall came down. Nations are joining in treaties and agreements to share resources. The old ways of selfishness, suspicion and separation are crumbling under the insistent pressure of the increasing frequencies on our planet.

The increasing vibration and light in our world are stimulating new areas of the brain. This allows creative thinking to come more easily. We will see many new discoveries and inventions that support a streamlined yet simplified life style in our future.

If you feel none of this affects you directly, you are wrong. Everything and everyone influences everything else. If you feel you no longer have the time to go to a mall to shop for household goods, you will become more intent on locating mail order catalogs, or shopping the Internet. Businesses will find ways to improve their mail order capabilities, and become more serious about making their presence known on the Internet to supply your demand.

More opportunities for working from home via personal computer will become available. Since we will be slow to recognize how impossible it is to accomplish the typical workload in our shortened days, our workforce will cry out for relief. Removing the commute from a worker's day serves two purposes. The extra time restores some quality to his life, and also saves the cost of office space for his employer.

Many of these changes sound as if they are driven by the almighty dollar: consumers shifting their shopping methods, manufacturers shifting their focus to match the change. It just sounds like good old Capitalism at work. I believe it is more basic than this.

The most successful companies have a mission statement with which the organization's employees can identify. Everyone in those businesses feels the passion for their common goals. After all, a company is nothing more than a group of individuals who have come together for an agreed purpose.

A purpose of "making money" does not capture any true passion in people. Individuals may identify dollars with power, and yearn to climb to the top of the heap, but this is an empty passion. Money is only a symbol for the exchange of energy. It is a natural by-product of the activities of a group of individuals passionately working toward perfecting their purpose.

Companies will not secure prolonged success if their focus is on how to trick people out of their money. More consumers are becoming sensitive to their manipulative intent, and avoid them. Instead, the company with a service or product in which it believes, striving to keep it available to those consumers it feels could benefit, will find itself at the right place and time to fulfill the consumers' needs. Here the exchange of energy (goods for money) will flourish because of the clarity and purity of intent.

Nature's Example

Although interconnectedness and the flow of energy exist everywhere, it is most evident in Nature. When you walk through the woods, every plant and tree is where it is because the seed found the correct amount of soil, water and sun to flourish. All of the plants, trees, rocks, air and streams seen together produce a scene that evokes a particular feeling. Although it is made up of separate elements, they exist and evolve in relation to one another. There is a balance of energy that quietly binds the green hillside into the wholeness of an environment.

To this energy are drawn more mobile creatures that find it a valuable place to be. They may come here because they feel at home. They may find an abundance of smaller creatures on which to feast, the energy of the smaller moving to the energy of the larger creature. Whatever their agenda, they would not have chosen to walk, slither or fly there unless the scene was in accord with their own energy.

If a fire comes through and destroys what has been, a new environment will begin to evolve as plant and creature are attracted to this "cleared" place. Even the event of the sweeping forest fire would not have come to this place, if the energy there did not draw to itself this extreme catalyst of change.

It has always jarred me deeply when I witness new highways being constructed, especially when many trees and plants are being removed in the process. The natural energy of the area is drastically and forcibly changed in a very short period.

Ironically, such changes are caused by the transportation requirements of many people moving further from their jobs to be closer to Nature. To support the greater numbers of commuters, the highway planners draw their lines across maps. They decide on which easement will allow the growing population to commute more easily to their jobs from outlying areas. A bit more of Nature's natural energy is altered in a flurry of human activity.

I have often fantasized about a heavy equipment operator who looks lovingly upon the timber before his huge machine's iron claw. In my imagination, he addresses the trees personally, asking that they forgive the harsh treatment about to befall them. He honors them for their purpose of being, and promises to do his work swiftly with reverence for their essence that is being destroyed. He then works on through the project, day after day, making it his pleasure at every opportunity, to adjust his tasks so that the greatest beauty in concrete form will remain where Nature's beauty once stood.

Beauty is like a lubricant that helps energy to flow smoothly into natural forms. Every time someone does the simple act of picking up a piece of trash from a patch of grass, the beauty available to be appreciated is increased. The vibration of the scene is heightened. The good intent of the person kind enough to remove the blemish nourishes what is there. The whole of our world is improved.

If we have awareness of Nature in our heart, our choices of action will be in harmony with Nature's evolution. Each of our choices will move in this accord. As we fall in synch with Nature's flow, all of life moves with this gentle, sureness; the Highest Good is done.

The Flow of Energy

Although you may not feel them now, in every moment of your life there are currents of energy flowing through the events as they unfold. It is a synthesis of the energy of the elements at work: the actors involved, the site at which the event is occurring, the time of day, the position of the planets, and a thousand other subtle bits. Every element has its own energy signature— a unique vibration or pitch. When these elements come into interaction, the harmonies and dissonance between them energize the dynamics of what unfolds. The energy in the words spoken, and the actions of the actors, also toss more ingredients into the soup of the moment.

This movement and interaction of energies are at a very subtle level. It takes patience and practice to be able to sense this energy movement directly. These currents of energy flow through every event we experience.

Almost everyone has had experience with currents of some kind, such as currents in the air as wind, or in water. If you have ever swum in the ocean, perhaps snorkeling off a reef, you have felt the currents of the water upon your body. You knew naturally that it affected your progress, and you had to consider its movement as you chose your direction.

Lee and I bought a canoe recently and have begun paddling. I had been around powerboats before, but the more subtle aspects of hull in water are much more evident with the canoe. We have a particularly favorite trip that runs six or eight miles downstream on the Hillsborough River, through some beautiful Florida wilderness. No white waters, but the current flows quite rapidly on some sections. I have found it most intriguing that as you approach turns where the current is strong, you must start turning the canoe very early to allow the river current to move the craft efficiently around the corner. It is not one's first inclination to do so.

As Lee encouraged me to go against my initial feelings, I found the current's assistance bringing to my awareness a new way of sensing the connection of the canoe and water. My challenge is to learn how to surrender my ego's opinions to the natural course of least resistance, as canoe and current wind peacefully through the cypress and water plants.

Our broader physical experience with currents and flow, can give us clues on what to watch for in the more subtle realms. Everything that happens on our planet is created through the movement of energy in the thoughts and intent of those in residence. Even something as broad reaching as the United Nations was nothing but a thought in the mind of one person. Once shared, this thought grew and blossomed forth as it caught the ear and passion of others. The energy of the idea attracted the energy of those who became involved in its founding.

Remodeling one's home, starting a study group, forming a new company or a new nation from part of an old—all these things begin as a thought form of energy in the mind of one actor. If the time is right, other actors will be excited by the idea, give over part of their own fertile mind to nurture the thought, and feed it energy to encourage its growth.

Answers to questions around how and when to express the idea will begin to be found. Materials necessary for its success, whatever they may be, will become available. What is happening is that the energy of the idea is attracting these things together. For example, you decide to stop at a large building supply store where you find the perfect color of paint you had imagined only that very morning. This is the flow of energy at work.

The smallest physical action we initiate, moves into physical expression based on an idea. As one learns to ride these natural currents of energy, the flow in the actor's life becomes fluid. It is like riding a river in a craft that is well known.

Sometimes these thought-currents may be swift, sometimes more gentle. There may even be times when one feels as if the river has widened into a lake. Here the depth of ideas take a while to formulate to the point at which they are ready to manifest. This most natural process of ideas flowing into physical expression is always at our disposal. It gives us a sense of effortless activity as our life moves along.

In recent years, a new art form has come into being: holographic images that can be framed and hung on your wall to intrigue and mesmerize your guests (and yourself). As you shift your vantage point before the image, it moves and changes. Perhaps an image of a young woman winks, or the image changes entirely into a different picture before your very eyes. You know it is a static thing. It is a picture hanging on the wall. But somehow, it has encapsulated a changing scenario that is always waiting to replay upon your next visit. There appears three-dimensional depth that belies its flat surface neatly tucked into an ordinary frame.

The amazing properties do not stop here. If you were to remove the frame, place it upon a table and sit before it, you could move your eyes across it appreciating the full image. If you were to snip a small fragment from one corner and lay it back in its place, nothing much has changed. However, pick up the fragment and slowly move it across the image, and something different would appear. As the small fragment (from one corner) is moved across the image, you would see reflected back to you, the portion of the image over which it is suspended. It no longer would reflect to you what it did while in the corner!

What has happened is the entire image is captured in every portion of the picture. Although each square inch performs the purpose of reflecting that specific position of the image, it still retains knowledge of the whole. This is a most amazing and fascinating art form.

I choose to feel these images were invented to remind us that we all carry the imprint of the Whole within our Beings. We are One with Divine Oneness. Yet, in our own individual way, we reflect one unique expression of that Whole from our current position.

Where we fit into the total production is a dynamically changing arena. The energies flowing through us, and the world that we create, move us to those places we are meant to be to express our unique spark. This grand dance in which we all participate is the most wonderful and exciting mystery of all.

SIX

How Can I Make
This All Real For Me?

THIS IS WHERE YOUR ADVENTURE can really take off! Once you accept the possibility of further areas of discovery beyond your physical world, the fun starts in finding ways to convince yourself of this truth. If this perspective is new to you, you will be amazed at how much has gone unnoticed before.

Each section in this chapter is offered so you can become aware of the variety of things available to sensitize yourself to a new way of viewing your world. Each section represents a different angle from which the Oneness of all things can be glimpsed.

Some of what will be presented will describe divination devices. Any of these things—cards, pendulums, astrology, etc.—have no power of their own. It is you who brings your God-spark magic into the interaction. Even though they are external physical things you can grasp and play with, the only purpose they serve is to amplify the information and knowledge already coming into you from your higher-self, guides, and Spirit. These things are merely tools to help increase your intuitive ability to sense your connection to the larger picture. Tools in a similar way that some PC software can help you gain a clearer understanding of your personal finances.

What follows is just an inkling of the adventures that await you. If any of these areas catch your eye, you will find many books available specifically written on each subject to satisfy your further curiosity.

One of the first things to do—especially if you have never done so—is to look up a metaphysical shop and go browse the shelves. It will be a treasure chest of tantalizing and unusual things to discover. There are books, crystals, cards, divination devices, stones, candles, chimes, incense, music, jewelry, classes and workshops, and shopkeepers who have experienced personally those things that you have just begun to understand you wish to explore.

Always remind yourself: all the things you see through your eyeballs are being brought to you by yourself. Your decisions are writing your script. Always take care to go where you are comfortable. Then, just enjoy what happens.

If you go to a store, and what you see or feel makes you nervous, check with yourself. If you are nervous because you do not know what you are looking at and you do not want to appear foolish, get over it. Do not waste your valuable time being concerned with what others will think. Remember, every actor is so busy with their own Play, they rarely have the time or interest to notice what is going on with another actor.

However if you are nervous with the surroundings—if something about the place leaves you cold—then move on down the road. It is important that the energies of any place

you visit often are in harmony with your own. When you find
a place that allows you to relax into your most natural state,
you can soak up a lot of information and knowledge through
your pores as well as your mind.

My suggested reading for you follows: **Enter your title here,**
by *your author here*. This book is the one that you notice on the
shelf. What attracts you? Is it the color of the cover? The size?
The position on the shelf? Or is it your higher-self nudging
you to something it is time for you to hear? Sometimes just
a skim at the store will be all that was needed. You will know
(as usual). You will be the only one who will.

You will find information anywhere and everywhere. Keep
your eyes open. It may be in a book on someone's coffee table.
You may find something on an empty seat on the bus. If it
attracts your attention, it is for you. Otherwise, you would not
have taken notice, or be holding it in your hands.

Become aware of spontaneous events as they are unfolding:
that book that attracted your attention from the shelf. You
might find yourself stopping in a grocery isle where you have
never stopped before: your body may need some nutrients in
the items there. You may decide to stop at a new restaurant:
look around, is there anyone there to whom you feel drawn?
Talk to them—just say hello—you may have information for
one other.

Always expect more than each situation would normally
provide. Do not operate from habitual patterns. When you are
operating in automatic, you are not really aware of what is happening. Remember to watch for, and expect, the unexpected.
Move willingly forward into new life opportunities that present

themselves. Follow your spontaneous impulses and see where they lead.

Also take note of coincidences that occur. Different events that bring you to the same *place* are trying to get your conscious attention. Look at them, and the more subtle symbols beneath the physically obvious. There are no such things as "accidents" or "mistakes." Each happening leads naturally to the next.

If your life appears bumpy and disjointed, you simply have not understood the underlying thread that is connecting these events. Even a silly piece of junk mail that catches your attention may have a sentence that provides an idea to clarify a pattern. Be sensitive to seemingly unrelated thoughts, gently offered into your mind. These messages provide information about what is unfolding, or the words would not have come to your notice.

Besides spending all your extra change on cool things to take home and play with, or watching the subtle events as your life unfolds, there are many fun exercises you can use to snoop into your subtle inner world.

Creative Exercise

I played with the following exercise early in my awakening. It is designed to allow one to glimpse the unlimited nature of one's creative powers. I was living in Houston at the time, and the sky was perfect: lots of small puffy clouds that drifted by slowly. However I must admit, when this exercise was first described to me, I doubted I would get any results.

To start, sit somewhere you can easily see the sky, and get comfortable. Look up at the clouds and pick out a small one separate from the rest. The object is to cause the cloud to disappear! The nice thing about clouds is you can stare at them for a long time and they do not care. I am also confident that one need not feel guilty about killing a cloud.

The technique I found most successful was to pretend the blue sky was a hot griddle, and the white cloud a bit of lard sitting on it. I would look at the cloud, and begin to *know* that the hot sky griddle was melting the cloud into nothingness. As I focused my attention on melting the cloud, I would start seeing blue where the cloud still was. When I looked normally at it after thirty to forty-five seconds, I could see the cloud was getting thin. After a couple of minutes, it was truly gone.

Well, I am very much like you. I saw the cloud go away, and the clouds that were next to it were unchanged. But I probably had to melt several hundred clouds before I began to believe it was my intent that caused the gathering water vapor to disperse.

I found it fun to watch the variation of results when using different frames of mind during the exercise. How long did it take if I made myself quite emotionally neutral? How long if I made a heart connection with the cloud, expressing my love for it and holding it lovingly as I caused its form to change? I quickly noticed that if I tried very hard, it took the longest, or did not work at all. Such intense concentration usually left me with a slight headache.

Even though our natural abilities are forgotten once in physical form, they are always available for our use. They are above all else: *natural.* When one forces mentally, trying too hard, our natural abilities cannot flow, and success is less frequent. Knowing this, use it like biofeedback. When you try something and it works well, notice how you felt. It will give you information about how your personal subtle skills are most easily engaged.

Discovering and working with one's creative powers is most amazing. I have long remembered an experience I had when I was seven or eight years old. The 4th of July was approaching. Each year our family went to a nearby lake where my aunt and uncle lived. We would all have a picnic together, swim, fish and enjoy the day until it got dark. Then we would gather together to watch the fireworks display. It was always great fun!

This particular year, the weather in the Seattle area had been rainy and cold. I remember clearly asking with great intensity to have one warm sunny day on the 4th. On the morning of the 4th, the clouds were gone. The sun was warm, and our day was as filled with fun as I had imagined. The weather for the next day, and the following week, was again cloudy, wet and cold.

I cannot tell you why I felt this way, but I was very sure my request was directly responsible for the one-day oasis of sun. I may not have been alone. There may have been others who pointed their intentions for the same event. But whether one or one hundred actors focused desire, I felt sure the weather's change was a direct result.

Chinese Exercise Balls

This is something you might wish to explore. Chinese exercise balls come in a set of two balls in a variety of sizes, patterns, colors and materials. The primary use is to hold both in one hand, palm up. By manipulating your fingers, they will circle one another while resting against each other. Each ball is constructed with a hollow center where a toning device is located. As they roll around in your palm, they make bell-like sounds you can hear and feel in your hand and forearm. They are great for stress reduction, as well as stimulating the flow of energy throughout the body. If you like to play with them, you may find yourself spontaneously creating new personal techniques.

My original set has a dark green background, is made of a hard rubber-like material, and rings with deep resonance. They each have a picture of a dragon and clouds on them. One depicts a blue land dragon with feet and a red mane like a lion, the other, a red sky-dragon with wings. However soon after starting with them, I found I had a problem. As I rotated them in my right palm, my left hand and forearm became impatient. My attention would be pulled to the empty hand saying, "When do I get my turn?" No longer than one minute after the balls were transferred to the left, my right hand and forearm were pulling at my skirt saying, "Is it our turn yet?"

The solution was inevitable: a second set of balls. However, even as I mentally congratulated myself for cleverly resolving the issue, I found the solution becoming more complex. The new set was smaller and metallic with soft pink, blue, gold and silver swirling in their surface. I found both hands preferred the first set!

The eventual solution has satisfied all. My right hand starts (I am right-handed) with the beloved original set. When my left hand can wait no longer, the balls are transferred there, and my right hand works the newer set. Since the metallic balls are heavier and require greater muscle control to move smoothly, my left hand yields to the superior dexterity of the right. All is peaceful again.

Although this battle of wills within one's own body seems absurd, it is only an example of what might be noticed once one becomes willing to be consciously aware of such subtleties. We carry cellular memories in the muscles and bones of our own body. I suspect this rivalry and separative attitude was left over from those early days in elementary schools. This is when the question, "Which hand was going to be used to write?" was given too much attention. My two friends at the ends of my arms had forgotten they were two parts of the same whole (as we all can do). Now each hand can enjoy the pleasure found by the other, as well as its own, as each hand gently rotates and holds "the music."

Pendulum

Another fun device to play with is a pendulum. What it amounts to is a small weighty object tied at the end of a string or light chain. If you like this device, over time you will perfect the exact materials or colors you prefer. My favorite pendulum is made of a beautiful dark wood from the Brazilian rain forest, suspended from a fine yet strong black thread. Pendulums made of small quartz crystals are usually readily available at your favorite metaphysical shop.

Use: Sit or stand in a quiet place where you can hold the end of the string, while the weighted object at the end is unrestricted. Hold the end of the string as still as you can, perhaps supporting your arm down to the elbow against your body.

Ask yourself: "Show me what means YES." After a brief time the pendulum will begin a specific movement: back and forth, to and fro, clockwise circle, etc. It will establish one pattern that will mean "Yes" to you. Everyone finds his or her own movement.

Then ask "Show me what means NO." Again in a brief time, the pattern made earlier will change to a new pattern. Take your time. When you are satisfied the patterns are clear, you will have established a communication with your higher-self, your guides, with Spirit. You have a tool of which you can ask Yes or No questions to amplify subtle answers from your heart and beyond.

For example, if you have two jobs to choose between, write each down on a blank piece of paper and hold the pendulum above each. Ask in your own words, which job is best for you. Even if the pattern is "Yes" above each, there will probably be more energy, or greater movement, above one than the other. Of course, the job suggested may not be the one you expected. It may pay less or be in an industry in which you have no experience. But if you are comfortable with your pendulum's message, it will be suggesting which opportunity is most in line with your life's purpose.

If you are thinking of moving, hold it above the various areas on a map. Ask for guidance to a location most appropriate for your growth. Your pendulum will indicate Yes or No above your projected choices.

If your restlessness has broader boundaries with no known direction, pull out a map of your country, or of the world, and slowly move it around the land masses. There may be many areas where the response is neutral, as well as definite areas where the Yes is strongest. Also take careful notice of those areas shown as NO!

Many people find the pendulum to be an inconsistent tool. Be aware there will be days when you just do not *feel* the answers your pendulum is providing are accurate. On the days you feel this way, you will be correct. You will always know the quality of the information coming to you.

So, before you quit your job and move to Nome, Alaska, test your pendulum results against your heart and body sensations. When your body responds with quiet calmness, enjoy: your pendulum is amplifying information from your inner worlds for your Highest Good.

If when you first try your pendulum you get no movement, do not be concerned. You must first come to a point where you acknowledge the possibility of information coming to you in this way. Your subconscious fears or beliefs can easily stop the movement from materializing. If you get nothing, just set it aside for some time and try it again later (weeks, months, whenever). Just do not be surprised if one of those attempts finds life at the end of your string!

Cards

While living in Houston, I wanted to find a set of Tarot cards to use for personal divination. As I stood before the large selection of tarot cards in a metaphysical shop, I heard a woman's voice say, "OOPS!" and felt a bump on the back of my left ankle. Knowing there is no such thing as accidents, I leaned down and picked up *The Way of Cartouche* by Murry Hope.

I had been bumped to awareness by a book of instructions and twenty-five cards based on Egyptian energies. As I skimmed the book, enjoying what I read, I understood this was what I had come to the store to find. I just had not known it.

I still use this set of cards. While shuffling the Cartouche cards thoroughly each morning, I ask "What are the energies at work in my life today?" Then I lay them out in my own version of the star spread. I am looking for clues to help me be more sensitive and consciously aware of what lesson material is flowing in my life each day.

What I like best about these cards is they are quite simple (only twenty-five cards), and they lack the heavy tradition of other tools, such as tarot. Simplicity has always attracted me.

Another favorite of mine is the deck of fifty-four small (⅞" × 2¼") *Angel Cards* from Drake and Tyler (1981). Each card has a word written in a lovely calligraphic hand, along with angels pictured symbolizing the energies of the word. Such words as Light, Spontaneity, Love, Freedom, Understanding, Forgiveness, Simplicity, Healing, Humour, Adventure, Play, Willingness, Flexibility, Tenderness, Expectancy, etc. provide a full spectrum from which to choose. I draw several cards from a small pouch while asking "What words are appropriate for me on this day?" I then spend ten or fifteen seconds studying each, letting my Being absorb the energies revealed. As the day progresses, and later in the evening, I enjoy looking back to see how these energies appeared in what had happened.

Although the words separately may have a certain English meaning, their combined energies can evoke a feeling or meaning that goes beyond the separate dictionary connotations.

The understanding pops into a three-dimensional picture/feeling that gives you new insight into the day's events. This forms just one more clue for reading between life's lines.

A dear friend of mine selects one Angel Card, and leaves it out where she can see it. Several days, even weeks may pass. She does not draw another card to replace the first until she feels done with understanding why the first card presented itself for evaluation.

You will probably find your cards seem to take on a personality of their own. On some days, they may not want to shuffle at all, almost as if they are stuck together. On other days, they will tumble all over each other, making it hard for you to hang onto them. Sometimes when you reach to draw a card, it will almost jump into your hand; or it may cozy up to the card next to it and simply defy your grasp.

There is an endless supply of divination tools, in the form of cards, I Ching, Healing Runes, etc., all available for your personal perusal at metaphysical shops. If you meet someone with whom you feel in synch, they may use a divination device that proves to be one of your own favorites.

Most of these tools come with instructions. However, once you understand their suggested usage, always work with suggestions and ideas that come up in your mind. Modify your usage as feels right to you. Each person is unique, and your own style of interacting with a tool may lead you to quite a different technique than those presented by the original designer. Follow your intuition, no matter how odd it might seem to your rational mind.

I advise some self-control when working with divination tools. Focus your questions and attention only on a short period into the future. There is no point in looking too far down the road. By the time your life dynamically arrives, the question you asked years before will have little bearing. Also, you would not want to project strong opinions about what you expect will be happening. This will create an intent that limits the outcome to only that which your current perceptions can imagine. Remember, your creative abilities are always at your disposal.

The furthest ahead I work is two months. Every other month I lay out a horoscope spread of Cartouche Cards to understand the energies in each area of my life. I find it a fine stabilizer in case life gets too hectic, and I drift off-center during this time span. Looking at an overview of the two-month period helps me settle down and regain perspective and balance.

Numerology

Numerology is a fascinating discipline. It uses the varying vibrational frequency energy in our basic numbers (1, 2, 3, 4, 5, 6, 7, 8 and 9) to reveal meanings in things. Our lives are filled with numbers (phone numbers, social security numbers, dates, time of day, days of the week, etc.), and with proper nouns (names of people, cities, states, addresses, etc.). The letters in these words can be reduced to the numbers they represent. The root numerological value of each letter in our alphabet is shown in the following table:

A	J	S	=	1
B	K	T	=	2
C	L	U	=	3
D	M	V	=	4
E	N	W	=	5
F	O	X	=	6
G	P	Y	=	7
H	Q	Z	=	8
I	R		=	9

The basis of validity in Numerology rests on the truth that there are no mistakes or accidents. The full name you are given at birth, best denotes your overall energies and purpose in your lifetime. If you change your name during your life, by marriage or personal preference, the change in the numbers derived will give you information about how your energies are shifting as you evolve. Each letter in your full name (including middle name) reduces to a numeric value from the above chart. Then the results of each letter can be added to give your Destiny number. It is through experiences expressing the energies represented by this number that your greatest growth occurs.

Every number greater than nine can be arithmetically broken down into a single digit number, by adding the single digits of itself together. For example, the number 973 would be: $9 + 7 + 3 = 19$, then $1 + 9 = 10$, then $1 + 0 = 1$. The number one is the numerological representation of 973. As you work with deriving numbers, you will find some shortcuts that yield the same results. For example, you can discard or ignore the figure 9 in any number. 1996 derives to 7: 1 + 6. The same answer as 1 + 9 + 9 + 6 = 25, 2 + 5 = 7.

There are also prime or divine numbers that should not be broken down any farther. If a complex number or name reduces to 11 or 22, this number stands as the results.

Following is the brief explanation of the energies of each number based on my personal feelings. The names of planets shown in parenthesis show which planets share similar energy. As you seek out further information on Numerology, each number will take on a personal quality that will allow your discernment to come alive.

1 = The masculine, projective force of Creation. It is a strong, confident energy that marks the explosive instant when something at the wispy edge of form, takes on momentum to move from thought into manifestation. (Mars, Aries)

2 = The female, receptive aspect in Creation. It is a soft yet persistent energy that supports and nurtures. Without this energy in place, nothing could move into manifestation. (Moon)

3 = The convergence of male and female (1 + 2). It is a heroic energy that takes responsibility for, and champions the cause coming into manifestation. It is the adventurer who, if true to his own nature, moves confidently and swiftly to do well what must be done. (Jupiter)

4 = Is the essence of reflection upon reality, of WHAT IS. Great discernment marks strength of purpose, showing stable and reliable progress. Although this energy may be perceived as delays, there is more precisely a caution in viewing thoroughly, and knowing accurately what is unfolding. (Saturn)

5 = Involves a great deal of mental activity. There is a focus on interaction, inspired by a sense of community and fellowship. The individual becomes involved in and expressed through his interrelationship with others and his environment. Life is active, filled with many adventures. (Mercury)

6 = The number of balance and harmony. All extremes transmute into the balance point expressing the blended elements of positive and negative, yin and yang, etc. There is a great deal of tolerance, understanding that all people have their place in the total scheme of things. (Venus)

7 = Energies flowing with an awareness and acknowledgment of the Universal Oneness as basis of existence. It is the number of spiritual and metaphysical studies. Direction is accepted readily from intuition. The energy crosses the physical barrier to integrate Spirit with Mind and Body. (Uranus, Neptune) (This is my Destiny Number, derived from my full name at birth.)

8 = The number of material success. Those working in this energy have a great deal of success due to their abilities

to see clearly both the forest and the trees. Further, they have the desire to move forward energetically to bring into manifestation those ideas they know to be sound and prudent. (Sun)

9 = The number of service. Those expressing this energy have "been there, done that." They have come to understand that through a focus of service to others, a point of completion is achieved. This allows a return to the ONE, setting the stage for a new cycle to begin. (Neptune)

Just enough to make you dangerous! Play with names, phone numbers and such. Convert them to their root number and see how the energy of the number relates to that of the item.

Astrology

Astrological interpretation is another area that can give you scrumptious clues about what you have planned for yourself this time around. You may even find such fascination with astrology that you choose to take classes to learn how to prepare and interpret charts for yourself and friends. PC software is readily available to do the calculations for you.

As I move through my life, I have found that the style of interpretation presented by the various astrologers I have selected has fit my needs at each point. Remember, you choose the source from which you seek information. You will instinctively select the individual who best fits your needs at the time. You are simply looking through the interpretations of someone else, to hear what it is time to hear from your own higher-self.

Astrology works with many different astronomical elements, bringing them into a context that reveals energy interactions. These serve to reflect your perceived experience of your life.

The astrological chart itself is divided into twelve Houses, or areas, of your life. These areas focus on such things as your personal self, money and values, your home, personal and group relationships, your work, your friends, your interactions with the community and the world. Planets in our solar system, as well as the sun and moon, have attributes and energies that are unique. The twelve astrological signs also have energies and attributes that are unique to each.

Your astrological birth, or natal chart, represents the positions of the astronomical bodies at the moment of your birth. To calculate an accurate chart, you need your date and time of birth (preferably from a birth certificate), and where you were born. This dictates your position in space. The chart examines this point in relationship to all the planets' positions.

When you slid onto the Stage for your first breath, each area of your life was in a particular astrological sign. Each planet was positioned in only one house, in one specific astrological sign. The relationship between the planet's position at your time of birth form energy aspects that follow you throughout your life. It represents your blueprint, an expression of your Play's outline you created before birth.

Each person is born with his or her Sun in one astrological sign. The old "What is your sign?" pickup line comes from this Sun sign. The energy of your sun sign is the most apparent facade others see. However, there are many different factors that quickly color you into more subtle shades.

In what sign was your moon when you were born? These energies affect your emotional nature, help shape the relationship with your mother, and affect how you nurture yourself.

What astrological sign was on your ascendant at birth? This is the sign lying on the leading edge of your 1st House as you move around the astrological chart in a counterclockwise direction. This colors the position from which you view the world, and how you perceive yourself.

Even if someone matches you in Sun, Moon and ascendant signs, your variations from one another will be evident, since there are so many variables considered in the total chart.

The most similar person you will ever find will be your twin, if you were born with one. Many people born together with siblings will experience a special connection and similarities in interests. Even being born an identical twin does not make souls the same; each has their own story line. However, each will figure predominantly in the other's Play, or they would not have chosen to come in together.

At each birthday, a variety of astrological charts can be prepared. These focus more specifically on what energies you are working with for the upcoming year. What is revealed is the timing you chose, to help create particular focuses in your life. If you are experiencing strong emotional feelings, it can help to know an aspect is in effect that is exaggerating your emotional reactions, and that it will be passing in two months. With this information, you can become more patient with the feelings. It gives you the composure to look honestly at why it is happening, and what you can learn during the transit.

By comparing natal charts of two people, compatible aspects, as well as incompatibilities, can be identified. An experienced astrologer can even tell you the best times to sign contracts and form businesses.

It is very important to always recognize your own responsibility in these matters. It is your life. You are simply looking for some clues to help yourself in understanding and synching up with your life's purpose. It is not usually appropriate for an astrologer to use this information to interpret your life for you. Their skill lies in interpreting the energy synthesis created by the various planets' angles to one another, in various signs, in various houses of your life. The understanding of how this fits in with what is unfolding in your perceived experience, is best left to you and your heart. If an astrologer suggests ways this energy might manifest in your life, use the information as an example of interpretation. Then follow your own heart to your own understanding.

The phases of the moon are other subtle energies that can be useful to track. When a new moon occurs, a cycle is starting. During this period, it is an excellent time to begin working with a new idea or project. You might gather information and slowly form a manifestation that would crescendo toward completion at the full moon. This is a very successful way of working with this cycle.

On the waning moon, from the full moon to the next new moon, is a period of reflection and evaluation of what has been accomplished. It is a time to rest and prepare for the next waxing cycle to begin.

Many people set some time aside on the days of the new and full moons to formalize their plans in a personal ritual. As they look forward to the next cycle, they also give thanks for all that was learned and experienced in the cycle ending. To speak of such things aloud affirms your cooperative existence with all that is. It allows you to breakdown resistance in your body and mind so a more grand view of life can be experienced and expressed.

Another fun aspect of the moon to watch is called "void of course." The moon travels around the earth very quickly. It travels from one astrological sign to the next about every two and one-half days. It completes its cycle around the Earth, moving through all twelve Houses, after twenty-eight days.

After the last aspect between the moon with any other planet is completed, the moon is said to be "void of course" until it enters the next astrological sign. Most times this is a relatively short period: a few hours, perhaps during the middle of the night. However, occasionally it is an extended period of a day or more. It is a time when trying to start something new encounters more resistance than usual. It just cannot get rolling.

There are astrological calendars available that give you moon phase and sign information. It can be fun to observe how these energies affect what people are doing. Next time you have a day when everything is nutty—things are going wrong and you feel as if you are on a treadmill to nowhere—take a peek at your calendar and see what is up with the moon.

As you note the flavor of each day's activities, and cross-reference it to the astrological sign in which the moon is found, you will begin to develop a feeling for the energies that you experience in each sign. Perhaps you notice that during the sign of Libra, your relationships with loved ones run more smoothly. Knowing this, you can discuss a difficult subject when the moon is in Libra, thereby coming to an amicable resolution with a minimum of distress.

One planet that can cause us fits is Mercury: the planet of communication. Every three months, Mercury goes retrograde for the next three weeks. Retrograde means the planet appears to be moving backwards as viewed from our position in space. During its time of retrograde, communications and travel can become particularly difficult. It is far easier to have misunderstandings or botched up travel plans during this period.

All you need to do is take special care. After making an appointment, have it read back to ensure it is correct. Call the airport and check on your flight. If you have an important conversation, paraphrase and say back what you heard to make sure the understanding is mutual. If you intend to sign a contract, review it carefully—better yet, put off signing until Mercury has gone direct in the Heavens again!

You do not have to change your life based on what someone says about particular planets. But you may want to keep loose track of when these planetary occurrences are happening, to watch for any impact in your daily life. You will probably notice some occurrences affect you more strongly than others. You are looking for how these subtle planetary energies interact with your own unique energy. Have fun with it.

Nature

While talking about the planets, we would do well to shift our gaze to dear Mother Earth. Many messages are offered from the abundance and activity found in Mother Nature to those who would listen.

As I have wandered my personal winding path toward understanding what God means to me, I have found it easiest to identify with the feminine aspect so evident in Nature. Nature's simple beauty and bounty have always produced a grand reverence in me. The knowledge that all, which is seen in such diversity, is constructed from the same molecules of matter, lends legitimacy to God's creative hand at work. To witness the life force in a lowly weed successfully pushing through three inches of concrete to find its way to the sun, fills my heart with wonder.

Each day, we all see various creatures going about their daily life. I sometimes envy the simplicity with which they naturally follow each moment's impulse into their next action. This exemplifies a natural way of being that has taken me many years to begin to understand. My style of living still feels awkward when compared to their natural flow.

Creatures that represent energy similar to your own will draw your attention, while another creature's presence would go unnoticed. Therefore, personal information can be found in which creatures you notice in your day. In what activities are they engrossed? What impression does their activity give you?

There is a beautiful book titled *Animal-Speak, The Spiritual and Magical Powers of Creatures Great & Small*, by Ted Andrews. It talks of the energies of the various creatures and plants.

Those that draw your attention may have attributes that amplify your own. Or, they may be pointing out aspects in yourself it is time to deal with or express.

Another treasure from our dear planet is those stones and crystals produced through natural evolution. What amazes me most is these glistening objects come from deep within the dark soil and rock of our planet. The clear symmetrically faceted Herkimer Diamond, found in Herkimer, New York, has its start within a hollow in a piece of granite! The colors and shapes of these abundant gifts from Mother Earth seem endless.

Metaphysical shops carry many of these treasures for your enjoyment. Here you will also find books, written by authors purely moved to share their subtle appraisal of the quality of energy amplified by each type of stone or crystal.

You will find certain stones and/or crystals attract you more than others. If you find several you really like, try putting them in a little pouch and wearing them at your heart. They can literally *feel good* to you, and their steady energy can strengthen your resolve to accept or release those things in your life whose time has come.

I find that the stones and crystals in my pouch need changing from time to time. The energy requirements of one's body change as one grows and evolves. What I will notice is a lessening of the impulse to wear my pouch. I will then find some quiet time, and lay out all of my pouch-size stones and crystals on a flat surface. Using my pendulum I ask over each piece, looking for those who would like to "ride in the pouch." Sometimes there are only a few. Sometimes the "Yes" appears over almost too many to fit. After placing them in the pouch together, I verify a strong "Yes" over the combined energy with the pendulum. After assembling the new combination of energies, my urge to wear the pouch returns to a loud reminder as I dress to go out.

When you slowly browse over these beautiful gifts from our planet in your favorite shop, I guarantee there will be some that absolutely attract you. Although my intention may be to keep the amount spent below a certain figure, the day I come upon a large piece that calls to me is the day I allow myself the luxury of its company.

You may also find that stones or crystals you find irresistible will leave your friend cold. The connection of the stone/crystal energy with your own unique vibration will be a very personal adventure.

A dear friend owned and operated a metaphysical shop in Florida. She had a very special, personal connection with her merchandise. She selected every item as if she were buying it for herself. Of course there were some favorites she held back until she could face parting with them. Her discriminating buying practices ensured a wonderful energy in her shop, and made stopping by a pleasure.

Quite often some gorgeous piece would attract me. She would merely smile and say, "I knew that was for someone special, I just didn't know who."

I once encountered a large piece of Amazonite at this shop: a beautiful light turquoise color with white areas running through it. As I held it, I was guided to hold it at my heart. Immediately, all feeling of stress flowed out of my body, and

I felt in perfect balance. I moved it out of my aura, and then back in, and felt a wash of balancing energy coming from the stone. I knew this large piece was going home with me!

Once you have opened your home to these beautiful gifts from Mother Earth, you will wonder how you got along without them. They are much like friends. You may find it intriguing to sit quietly, close your eyes, and hold a stone or crystal in the palm of your left hand. Focus on the sensations in your palm. You may feel warmth, a prickly feeling, or pulses from the piece. They may be very subtle, or perhaps quite pronounced. Your energy is reacting to the vibrations emanating from the stone or crystal.

Vision

With some practice, you can learn to relax your eyes and see things you have not noticed before. Observing our bodies gives us an opportunity to do just this. Besides an electromagnetic envelope close around our physical form seen as a grayish haze, there are additional layers or bodies that are more subtle, yet pulsating with flashes and swirls of color.

To exercise your sense of sight, you can practice viewing stationary objects or pictures. The 3-dimensional art that has become popular in recent years, can help you train your ability to shift your vision. These are the busy, colorful nondescript pictures that you view while softening your gaze. Once you achieve the correct perspective on the jumbled maze, a simple three-dimensional form designed by the artist will pop out at you. The image was always there, but it was not visible until you adjusted your focus.

To view the soft colorful aura around the physical body can take quite a bit of practice, so have patience with yourself. While your eyes look straight ahead, for example, at the forehead, shift your *attention* to an area at the side of the head above the shoulder. You do not look straight at the area around the body (different from the 3-D art technique).

Find a friend willing to experiment with you, or stand before a mirror to view your own form. The aura is most easily seen in subdued light against a plain, light-colored background: preferably a neutral tone of white or light beige. Once you begin to see things around your subject, you can adjust the level of light or color of the backdrop to suit yourself.

What you will likely see first, will be a whitish-grayish haze that stands out about three-quarters to two or more inches around the body. The thickness of this etheric portion of the aura depends on how well a person is feeling, whether they are tired or rested, etc. All living things are encased in this life force sheath. You can see this hazy halo around plants as well.

With further practice you will likely see pinpoint sparkles, almost like intense fire flies. These are bits of energy moving in the aura. Finally you will see translucent colors swirling around various areas of the body. The colors may be clear and bright, or more muddy. The clearer the color, the more clear the expression of the energy quality associated with the color will be. For example, a person experiencing and exhibiting anger will display a frenzied activity of bright, clear red. If the red is muddier, the anger is suppressed with less direct expression involved.

If dark areas exist in the aura, they suggest an area where the life force energy is not moving naturally. It could show the presence of a dis-ease. Many alternative health practitioners will use their ability to view the energy in the aura to help diagnose a patient.

The appearance of a troubled area in the aura can precede the manifestation of an illness in the physical body. Using clearing and healing techniques, an experienced healer can resolve the imbalance of auric energies to heal the dysfunction before it escalates into symptoms in the physical body.

When thinking in terms of vision, we could also say we are looking at the quality of our ability to observe. What do you see when you look into the mirror at yourself? You are looking at a reversed image of yourself. Your real left side is seen on your reflection's right side, and vise versa. Since none of us are perfectly symmetrical, the Being you view in the mirror is entirely unique. The mirror is the only place you can see this Being. He is as unique as you are yourself.

Pretend for a moment that the image before you is truly a visible form of your angelic higher-self. Look deeply into those eyes, and allow a sense of deep love to well up in your heart. Take the opportunity to speak to this gentle Being who looks back at you.

Ricky, our Eclectus parrot, loves to visit our bedroom. He stands in what we call the "hall of mirrors." Two walk-in closets face each other on a short hallway, each adorned with mirrored sliding doors. The mirror behind Ricky reflects himself back into the mirror in which he is looking. Back and forth the reflected image bounces, increasing the number of pretty green birds by one each time. As he and I look deeper and deeper into the countless reflections, I can imagine the bit of infinity that is at work before our very eyes!

Learn to look past what you habitually see. Look past the boundaries of objects as they appear in a scene. Is there a larger pattern formed by the position of a variety of things within your frame of reference? Are there other more subtle images formed by a composite of textures or colors you have overlooked before? Reach into your mind and tickle your imagination into playing with what is before you.

Many years ago, a friend and I were driving to work in Seattle. As we drove with the sun behind us, I looked into the distance where a freeway gradually descended from left to right above Lake Union. All we could see from our vantage point was the bright golden reflection of the sun off the windows while the cars moved slowly in heavy traffic. My mind suddenly released the knowledge of what I was seeing, and in its place I saw a fine wire suspended. Along the wire were slowly sliding drops of a viscous material like oil, glowing with a golden color. As I commented on the vision, my friend easily dropped into the same fantasy and we laughed at the fun of it.

Recently I was visiting a friend, and she was sharing her experiences with the M.A.P. (Medical Assistance Program) Conings she had been doing. These are very specialized meditations where direct assistance is received in bringing one's Physical, Emotional, Mental and Spiritual Being into balanced wholeness. This technique is presented in a book, *MAP, The Co-Creative White Brotherhood Medical Assistance Program*, by Machaelle Small Wright.

My friend was describing her sensory interpretations of the entities she was connecting with during these sessions. The name of one Being was Pan. She had been searching the Internet and other sources, trying to find out more information about this lighthearted master builder of the human form.

As I asked her to share her findings, she began to describe his physical appearance. I gazed past her at the wall beyond to focus more intently on her words. Out of the corner of my consciousness—almost going unnoticed—was a large area within my field of vision in which a superimposed image was being presented.

Once noticing, I shifted the attention of my focus from the wall to this area. Even then both were visible, as if overlaid on celluloid sheets. What I was seeing appeared to be pages being riffled in a large volume. Then it stopped at a page on which a drawing was presented. As her description continued, I said, "I see him! I can see he is holding and looking at a pipe." "What kind?" she asked, testing the accuracy of what I was reporting. "A musical pipe, straight with holes in it that he enjoys playing."

He looked to be mostly human in form, but parts of his anatomy appeared to be similar to an animal. Short horns protruded from his curly hair. Animal fur covered his lower body and most of his chest was bare. As I described what I was seeing, the image stayed—for at least ten seconds—then faded away. What I had described matched what she had learned from other sources. We both looked at each other in amazement and appreciation for this new adventure.

So transparent had the image been, I have since wondered how many such occurrences might have previously gone unno-

ticed? And how many more visions waited in my future, as
I became willing to notice.

Colors

Each color vibrates at a different frequency. The eye recognizes colors based on the vibration of the light received. When
you are looking at a rainbow, you are seeing a range of visible
light arranged so the lowest to the highest vibration lay out
side-by-side. Seven basic colors are discernible in the rainbow:
Red is the lowest vibration, next comes orange, then yellow,
green, light blue, indigo blue and finally violet, which vibrates
at the highest frequency.

Because Red is of the lowest, coarsest vibration, it radiates an
energy that exemplifies our physical third-dimensional world.
The lower the vibration, the more heat is present. At the other
end of the spectrum, heat gives way to a coolness and connection to the Higher realms.

Decorators often talk of cool or hot colors. This refers to the
vibratory rates of each color. There are certain colors that are
more effective than others in particular rooms, given the activities that occur in the room. You would not want to paint walls
red in a waiting room. It would become difficult to sit still and
have patience when the red vibration bombarding you was
asking for activity, and riling up anger at the length of time
passing. A cooler choice of color from the higher vibratory end
of the scale would soothe and relax. It could even alter the time
sense of those waiting, allowing the time to slip by far less
noticed.

If you were to get some construction paper from a hobby shop made in the clear colors of the rainbow, you can set up an experiment. Set pieces of the colored paper on a table, in the same order as they appear in the rainbow: red, orange, yellow, green, light blue, indigo, and violet. You may want to cut the paper into a simple geometric shape. A circle is best, because its boundaries are without any sharp angles, which can interrupt the energy flow. To give yourself a good neutral background, lay a sheet of white paper down before arranging the colored pieces.

Now, hold the palm of your left hand above the red, close your eyes, take some deep breaths and relax. *Feel* the color. After you have lingered over the red for a minute or two, move your hand on to the next color (orange) and feel it. Continue slowly moving on until you have felt your entire rainbow. The more you practice this exercise, the more feeling you will begin to sense. Some feeling will be in heat or coolness. There are other sensations you may detect, perhaps a prickly feeling or a pulsing sensation.

Once you begin to think you feel heat from the red, test it by moving your palm from the center of the circle to the white background. You will feel the much cooler white. If you move your hand slowly, you will actually feel the edge of the red circle pass across your palm!

Each color serves its own purpose within our Being. To be whole and well, our bodies need a balanced portion of all of the colors of the rainbow. And our bodies always know what is needed.

Try placing a small piece of each color in a container. Then in the morning, ask "What color do I need this day, to balance my body in perfect health?" Without looking, reach into the container and draw a color. Whatever it is, select the garments you wear that have this color in them. If you do not have any clothing of this color, carry the piece of paper or another object having this color in your pocket. You could also select your foods that day to match the color presented. If you continually draw yellow and own no yellow clothing, buy a yellow T-shirt or another simple garment, and wear it when you can. These are very subtle adjustments for our well being, but they all help achieve balance.

Once you have become sensitive to the feeling of colors, you can reach into your container, draw a colored shape, and try to tell what color it is without looking. You may surprise yourself at the accuracy you can develop. You may even begin to sense similarities in certain colors, one with the other. Of course, if you expect to fail in your discernment, the Universe and your subconscious will gladly honor your intent.

When writing this book, I went to an office supply store to purchase a 3-ring binder, so I could carry the rough draft with me. The colors available did not seem appropriate. I settled on a light gray binder, and left it at that. Later I realized the gray made me feel several things about the work-in-progress that seemed absolutely appropriate. For example, it did not speak boldly with a theme or feeling of its own. It remained neutral, giving me the impression of drawing simple truths from objective observation of the colorful world around me. It also struck me as a midpoint between the Light (white) and Dark (black), producing a balanced viewpoint in the information presented. The gray color also spoke with humility, helping me honor the simplicity of the words that brought themselves together between its covers. It signified balance and calmness needed to be open and receptive for the information to come in.

Playing in Traffic

To bring yourself in line with Divine Existence, you can practice unconditional love. Traffic is a very peaceful place to interact with others. Everyone is all packaged up in their own environment, as we scurry about with our precious cargoes. I find it a fine time to view many actors, and practice unconditional love for the wide variety of Spirit's essences in physical expression. It is particularly valuable practice because most people are not at their best while pushing through traffic. If I can love them on the highway, I can love them anywhere! They are all family, on or off the roadways.

While driving in traffic, you can practice your observation and interpretation of symbols. Traffic may be flowing smoothly, extremely slowly, or anywhere between; there may be many cars or very few. The quality of the traffic flow is a message for you. The fun is in ferreting out the meaning.

In every moment, we are exactly where we need to be, or we would not be there. Everywhere we go, our energies are interacting with those around us. Like energies attracting like, while dissimilar energies are pushed away. The feeling of the traffic flow you are participating in, will hold interesting clues for you.

Sometimes the energy directly reflects your internal condition: if in a calm, accepting mood, traffic will likely move smoothly, even with many cars. At another time, it may be showing you an energy example of something in your life:

it allows you to view it objectively, outside the actual situation, to gain perspective. What is your traffic situation telling you? If you find yourself in heavily restrictive traffic congestion, look at your internal state. If you feel tense and angry, you are letting it get to you—matching its energy with your own. Forgive yourself for your anger and the traffic for the restrictions it is placing on you. Remember that you are where you need to be.

There is a reason for everything and no mistakes, even when you do not understand what it is. As you gain perspective and release your tension, you will likely see a change in the situation. Perhaps a clever detour route will pop into your head to release the brakes. If you are still stuck, be aware the delay is affecting the time at which you will reach your intended destination. It may serve the purpose of adjusting your time frame, so you cross another actor's path, meeting for the first time. Everything is always in Divine Right Order. So have patience, and look beyond the surface.

Once Lee and I were in our automobile, heading home from some errands. As is true in any urban area, our choices of which streets we could travel were never ending. Lee was driving, and as he approached a turn that would have taken us down a well-known arterial, a strong urge came up in me. I asked him to please take another route. Without question, he honored my request, and selected another way home. We arrived home healthy without incident. I will never know what problem, accident or unnecessary situation was avoided by his adjustment. All I knew was the importance of taking a different path home.

When in traffic, relax yourself and watch the cars around you. You will get a feeling when a car will be changing lanes. You will be picking up their intentions in your mind. You may get the feeling someone does not know *where* he or she is going. That is the actor that makes the sudden right turn from the left lane. They are the ones to give plenty of room.

Sensitize yourself to the energies surrounding you, and allow your inner guidance to chart a safe passage for you.

Breathing

When we are first born into this life, we have many natural attributes functioning normally. But our natural aspects become suppressed and forgotten, as we are taught by those older. Breathing can be one of these casualties.

As an infant, each actor breathes deeply, using all of his lungs. Air comes into the lungs as the diaphragm moves downwards and the abdomen balloons out. Air pushes out as the diaphragm relaxes to its normal position. However, breathing from the diaphragm can be replaced with shallow breath in the upper lungs, when we are taught to "Stand up straight" and "Pull in that stomach."

When you stand before a mirror and inhale, does your abdomen protrude? Do you only see movement about the shoulders and chest? If you see your abdomen moving, congratulations. You survived this limiting behavior. However, if your tummy stays tight and proper while your shoulders lift, you have a delightful awakening in store.

Lie down comfortably on the floor or a bed. Place one of your hands below your rib cage, just above your navel. Take a deep breath through your nose, while thinking of pushing out and up against your hand. When you have breathed as deeply as is comfortable, hold the breath for a slow count of three. Then breathe out through your mouth, pushing gently upward with your diaphragm while your hand rides along.

If this is a new sensation for you, then practice this for several minutes a day until it becomes less foreign. If this feels uncomfortable, do not worry about holding your breath to start. Work up to the count of three gradually. Your objective is to train your body to eventually take every breath into the deepest realms of your lungs. This technique increases your useful lung capacity, and takes in more oxygen and energy, or *prana*, with each breath. Your body's system can function at its optimum, as you provide it more of the cleansing and rejuvenating elements exchanged between the lungs and your blood supply. You are not well grounded in your physical body, unless you are taking deep breaths from the diaphragm.

You may also want to watch yourself when you become anxious. It is very common to involuntarily hold one's breath at such times. During a time of stress, the best thing you can do for yourself is to take some deep breaths. It restores your physical and mental equilibrium and balance. Your brain is one of your largest customers when it comes to oxygen consumers in the body. Watch for this habit of holding your breath, and lovingly break it when found with some deep diaphragmatic breaths.

Once you feel more at home with your breathing, there are some fun experiments you can do to **drink in energy** with your breath. It will help you to learn how to challenge your beliefs about the physical aspects of your body.

Go outside on a sunny day and stand on some grass. Close your eyes, and feel the warm sun on your skin. Take some slow, deep breaths, and feel the sun's energy coming into your nose, throat and lungs. It is a golden-yellow color, perhaps the consistency of honey, and stimulates your sense of well being.

Next, shift your attention to the top of your head. Here is your Crown Chakra, open and facing the sky like a funnel. It is an energy center that connects you with the higher vibration of the Universe. As you breathe in, feel this golden-yellow light being inhaled *through the top of your head*. As you are slowly filled with this golden light, feel this color energizing your body, breath after breath.

Next, shift your attention to the grass beneath your feet. Feel the pure and simple rhythm of the Earth providing your life-supporting environment. Feel the growth and life force in the grass under you. As you breathe in, breathe the gentle yet constant life force up *through the bottom of your feet*. Feel this unconditional love move up into your body. The color is green with (perhaps) a tinge of brown from the trees nearby. As this abundant life force moves up, and fills your body, it centers on your heart area. The warm golden light, from above, swirls playfully with the green energy gladly provided by Mother Earth.

Do not rush. Take your time, and allow the colors to move naturally in you. As you take slow breaths, notice the sensations and colors as they move in your body. You can feel the truth that you are not limited to this physical form. Your edges are permeable. The warm connection you are enjoying between Sun and

Earth flow through you as easily as you can flow out to them. You are coexisting with every part of the Whole.

Now there is no right or wrong about this. There is no need for such thoughts as "What do I do with the colors when I am done?" "How long are my breaths?" "Can I open my eyes?" Allow your natural inclinations to guide you. However your experience takes form, is what is right for you. Your guides will not let you become lost. You have protection and guidance whenever you want it. If you have concerns when you experiment with something new, ask "May nothing but the Highest Good come to me in that which I am about to do." If you feel uncomfortable, ask to be protected from any and all harm, and it is so.

Meditation

In addition to interacting with your exterior world, it is time you explore your inner world. Meditation requires nothing more than you, and a place where you can be undisturbed and physically comfortable. Whether you sit in a chair, on the floor, or lie on the bed or floor, the most important factor is that you are comfortable. You do not need any easy excuses for shifting your attention away from something coming up in your inner world.

Meditation is merely a shifting of awareness from the external to the internal. It has no rules. Everyone develops his or her own methods.

To achieve a meditative state, it may help to focus your attention on something specific, to quiet your busy ego-mind. Focus on the sound of your breath, or on the movement of air in and out of your lungs. You can start with touring your body slowly from toe to head (or head to toe), relaxing all the muscles along the way. Releasing tension from the body soothes any emotional or anxious feelings.

As you perfect your ability to shift your awareness from the external to your inner world, more information and seed ideas will come gently into your mind. Some people clearly see visions, like film clips; almost everyone will see colors and perhaps patterns. You might hear music, or feel someone is speaking the ideas coming into your mind from outside yourself. But once you quiet your ego's babble, everyone experiences *silence!*

Whatever is needed begins naturally flowing into you, once you learn to *willingly be within the silence.* If you are uncomfortable with silence, there are many audiotapes you can purchase. They will take you on guided meditations, until you become curious enough to create your own adventures.

Touching Your Guides

There is a lovely exercise offered in *Kryon—The End Times— Book 1,* copyright 1993 by Lee Carroll. The technique acquaints you with your guides: those (usually) invisible Beings who dedicate their time in loving service to your growth. The following is a quotation from this book:

> "When you are finished with this reading and you retire tonight, I challenge you with this exercise. I guarantee you will have results if you are sincere, for this is truth; and it will manifest itself as reality because of that. You will feel some of this new love

energy that I so often speak about. Please do the
following.

The exercise: With your eyes closed, imagine
yourself standing on a hill overlooking water. There is
no noise except that of waves or wind. Stay there until
you void your mind of everything earthly. If sounds or
music will help, then sing to yourself in your thoughts
to allow for peaceful thoughts. Slowly imagine the veil
of duality approaching you, and stopping just a meter
or so before you. If you cannot imagine this, then call
for it and it will come. It has to come when called.
Now stretch out both hands as in a welcoming
fashion to your guides on the other side of the veil.
You can do this actually, or just in your imagination,
but keep your hands outstretched and wait. In a few
moments you will feel your hands become warm, or
tingle slightly. This is the truth of your hands being
held! In addition, you will be aware of an
overwhelming sensation that will make you weep.
This sensation is one of joy and peace. The universe
is really there, and it cares about you. You will be
actually reaching through the veil, and can touch your
guides. Your guides are the closest entities in service,
and they love you dearly. They are there in *love service*
and will be very receptive and excited to communicate
with the 'rest of you' for the first time. Imagine their
feelings, that you would respect them enough to reach
out to them, for to them *you are the exalted one*, and
they are serving you.

Pause and revel in this feeling as your hands are being held, for through your imagination you are actually creating *thought energy* which allows for this new communication. Thoughts are real energy, and what you will experience is very real and not just in your own mind. While you are in this state of joy, all fear will vanish about anything earthly, and a 'love wash' will take place that will provide you with peace and wisdom about the events you must face during your (physical) expression. You may even feel that you are beginning to rise above the land. Do not allow for this contact more than about *three minutes,* for to do more will fatigue your soul and translate to you as mental strain the next day. Believe me, you will be aware of the contact for hours. The after-glow will stay with you. Do not do this more than *one time a day.* This is not a mental exercise for the purpose of positive feeling. What you are doing will be as real to you as anything you do during the day."

Once you experience the reality of your guides in loving service, and your higher-self as a loving partner, you will find a new perceivable depth or dimension in every scene in your physical life. You will begin to expect to glimpse the underlying meaning in every conversation, every event. Your life will become alive and turn into a perpetual adventure.

As you welcome Divine presence into your every moment, the love that flows into you will overflow and become evident in your every choice of thought, word and deed. You become more enlightened: more filled with light. People around you witness your light in every ordinary thing you do. By working with and refining yourself in expression, you are helping the planet and every creature living upon it. It is the highest service you can provide to Humanity.

Tell Me About My Body— What Am I Made Of?

THE PHYSICAL BODY YOU EXPERIENCE through your senses is only a small part of your entire Being. Not only is there far more than is readily observable, but it is through the more subtle components and functions that your life essence is connected into the Whole of Creation.

Your physical form begins within the body of your mother. It is nourished and supported by the soul essences of you, your mother and your father. There are also divine Beings who specialize in assisting during prenatal time. They ensure that the physical form develops to meet the highest level of service in carrying our hero on his life's quest.

If there are birth defects, all concerned are aware in advance, on a soul level, and have agreed to these special conditions. If there is death in the early years, this too is planned before conception, and serves the growth of mother, father and child.

The molecular elements of which your body is constructed are the same as all plants and animals on our planet. What makes you YOU is the soul's consciousness—the natural

YOU—resonating within your body's physical structure. It is your soul's presence that retains the form.

Upon death and the soul's departure, the body begins to break down and return to the raw materials abundant in Nature. These particles continue to decompose to their most basic aspects. Then, another consciousness creating a physical form, attracts them into interaction with other simple components. The process of birth (of a new form) begins again.

Even as your physical body breathes, sleeps and partakes of nutrients, the molecules forming your every part are exchanged and refreshed. Yet even with the constant change at the molecular level, you still maintain a continuity and self-awareness.

At the subtlest end of our personal energy spectrums, tendrils of consciousness interact with the Earth's electromagnetic template. We are always in the perfect place for us. All of the positive and negative polarities have interacted with our own electromagnetic system, to form a balance in our current physical location. As the polarities within our immediate locale change, we feel encouraged to move to a new location. Depending upon the degree of shift, the new location may be in the same room, or far across the continent. We vary our electromagnetic balance within ourselves, as much as move our legs, to travel from one point to the next. We each operate without conscious knowledge at a grand and complex level within the Universe.

Chakras

For a very long time, Humanity has had seven major chakras, or energy centers, within his physical body. Also, hundreds of secondary chakras throughout the body focus and receive or put-out energy to a lesser degree.

The major chakras are seated into a perpendicular line, approximating the location of the spine. The nerve bundles in the spine carry electrical messages that make this conduit the most concentrated energy pathway in our body.

Each chakra forms a cone shaped energy vortex at its location. The large end of the cone of the first chakra, located at the end of the spine, points down at the Earth. Its counterpart at the top of the head, in the seventh chakra, points up toward the Heavens. The remaining major chakras each have two cone-shaped structures: one at the front of the body, the other at the back of the body. The large ends of these energy vortices point away from the body. The narrow ends of these vortices seat into the main power line, in the vicinity of the spine.

The first, Root or Base, chakra is located at the base of the spine. This chakra vibrates to the color red. It vibrates at the lowest frequency of the seven major chakras. This chakra maintains our connection into the physical plane of Existence. It is from this energy center that our physical form roots into the energies of our planet. It connects us to, and receives nourishment from, the Earth. This center is the basic structure on which the rest of the chakras build. It provides the security with which we experience being here. It operates on a very primal, sub-conscious level, without participation from emotional feelings or mental discernment. The element associated with this chakra is Earth, the sense is smell.

The second, or Sacral, chakra is located just above the pubic bone. The color of this chakra is orange. The energies it works with are the emotional and creative aspects of our Being. Our sexual energy and the quality of love we experience for sexual partners flows in this chakra. Our ability to give and receive pleasure is born here. Our sense of well-being is established here. The passionate beginnings of our creations start in this center. The element associated with this chakra is Water, the sense is taste. As our physically grounded energy moves up from the first chakra, this emotional center allows us to feel certain ways about the first chakra's energy.

The third, or Solar Plexus, chakra is located just above the navel. The color of this chakra is yellow, and it deals with our mental abilities and life force. Our personal power, sense of confidence and self-worth are developed and experienced from here. The element associated with this chakra is fire, the sense is sight. Using the discernment of our mind allows us to form opinions about energies coming up from the first and second chakras below. Our feelings and physical energies are then integrated into our statement of who we are in the physical world.

The fourth, or Heart, chakra is located slightly lower than mid-chest, at our physical heart. It is the most important of the chakras. The Heart chakra marks the midway point between the lower three and the higher three chakras. It bridges, and brings into integration, the lower (physical) and higher (spiritual) energies working in the body. The color this chakra vibrates to is green. Its energies are of love, compassion, forgiveness, healing and transmutation. We experience our feelings of brotherhood, peace and harmony through this center. The element associated with this chakra is air, the sense is touch. It is through this center that we feel our warm connectedness with all that is, when we gaze upon a beautiful sunset.

The fifth, or Throat, chakra is located at the throat. Its color is sky blue, and its energy deals with communication, will power and manifestation. The element associated with this chakra is ether, the sense is hearing. We take responsibility through this center for attaining what it is we want in life. When this chakra is operating smoothly, we are open to receiving all that is coming naturally to us, and we express ourselves clearly and easily. We feel nourished and satisfied. This energy center can very often be clogged with reluctance to share communication freely.

The sixth, or Third Eye, chakra is located between the eye brows. Its color is indigo blue. Our ability to visualize, form mental concepts, and to know one's truth is centered here. We experience imagination, intuition and knowing here. There is no element associated with this chakra, the sense is inner knowing. This energy center also forms a doorway into other levels of understanding our Universe. When one goes within, and sees the unseen, the images are processed here.

The seventh, or Crown, chakra is located at the top of the head. The color here is violet, the most subtle shade seen in the rainbow, vibrating at the highest frequency. We experience inspiration and beauty in this center. There is no element associated with this chakra, the sense is spiritual awareness. This chakra connects our totally integrated Being, including all the chakras below, with the Universe at large. It is the seat of our spiritual connection with Divine Oneness, and where we exchange energies with the Higher realms.

Along with the varying light frequencies focused in each chakra, musical tones climb the scale as we move from base to crown chakra.

Understanding and working with the energy in our chakras is the finest thing we can do for ourselves to promote our health. When our energy flows smoothly in all seven chakras, we experience a healthy, Whole condition. We are ready to move through each moment, freely able to focus our attention and awareness wherever appropriate.

There are many books available on this subject. I have found *Wheels of Life* by Anodea Judith a wonderful resource. Follow your guidance to those books most appropriate for you.

As we look across the seven energy centers at work, we see the same colors that we can observe in the rainbow in Nature, ranging from low to high frequency. Several years ago, I became very hungry to be able to bend white light into the clear hues of the rainbow, whenever I wanted. I searched until I came across a Plexiglas prism in a store selling telescopes and binoculars. Faceted lead crystals are also readily available, and can be hung where the sun might strike them and release these clear colors to enjoy. There is something very compelling about these clear visual tones, spreading themselves before your eyes from the sun's warm rays.

For physical exercise, I work out on a Nordic Track in the mornings. When I first began, I would set the timer to control the length of time involved. Finally realizing this was not what mattered, I shifted to a much simpler regime.

Closing my eyes while exercising, I begin working through the chakras as my physical form exerts itself. Starting at the base chakra, I focus on the location and color of this energy center. I remain here, sensing the fullness of it, until I feel a ball of energy form at its focal point and begin to move upward. I move my attention with this energy ball, stopping with full attention at the second chakra. After the appropriate length of time at each chakra is complete, I again feel the ball of energy form and move upwards. With each pause on this daily journey through my chakras come random understandings of the energy in each. I can feel the degree with which the energy flows freely. I become aware of possible areas of tension or blockage.

After reaching the top of my head, savoring the wispy violet energy of the crown chakra, I soften my gaze and look upon my body in total, enjoying the rainbow within. Then, the energy connection flows above my head and below my feet. I see bright points of light, focused in a pattern that completes a vision of an "energy wand" glowing vertically within my body.

I feel myself anchored in the Earth below, and to the Heavens above. Intersecting at these points below and above my body, I witness a golden egg-shaped form surrounding and protecting me. The Oneness of myself, connected with all that exists, lies warmly within my perception. Although this re-acquaintance ceremony has followed this format for some time now, the appreciation and sensations that come to my awareness are always fresh and appropriate for the day lying before me.

When on this visit-each-chakra journey, I always get a chuckle from myself when I reach the sixth (third eye) chakra. It reminds me of sinking a golf ball. You know, that satisfying little noise it makes as it falls into the waiting cup? My attention is on the ball of energy as it moves from the Throat Chakra toward my brow. When it arrives, it drops into a "hole" and disappears, and I go with it.

This chakra center can sense many dimensions of being. It is at this center that many images and energies—overlapping, interweaving, occupying the same space—can be sensed. The behavior of the energy ball I mentally follow is different at this center; it signifies the infinite possible places to be. It often feels as if I am drifting off into some foggy land of nowhere and everywhere, leaving my physical form dutifully moving to the pattern of the exercise equipment. Once this center's visit is complete, the energy ball reappears, as it hops out and rolls toward the Crown.

Coinciding with the seven major chakras are seven layers of our aura surrounding our physical form. The first layer of the aura—the etheric level—can be seen as a grayish haze close around our body. This first auric level is manifested by the energy in the first chakra. As the energies of each chakra rise in frequency and become more subtle, so do the ever widening auric layers surrounding our body manifested by its respective chakra.

Once you become familiar with the energies and locations of your Chakras, you can use this information to encourage wholeness in your Spirit, Mind and Body. Each Chakra is associated with specific organs and glands, usually located in the same area of the body. For example, if you are having problems with your bladder or circulatory system, your energy is not flowing freely and smoothly in your second Chakra. Someone experienced in working with the body's energy system can help you release any blockages, and restore the free flow of energy.

You can also feed your Chakras to focus assistance in regulating them to an open, healthy condition. The following shows the classes of food that agree in energy quality with each Chakra.

> First Chakra—meats, dairy products, proteins
> (beans, legumes).
> Second Chakra—fluids, juices, WATER.
> Third Chakra—starches, simple sugars.
> Fourth Chakra—vegetables.
> Fifth Chakra—fruits.
> Sixth and Seventh Chakras—cannot be fed, there is
> no physical equivalence.

Your body will naturally crave foods that feed a particular Chakra. You might notice a craving for salty foods, just as the Holiday Season in December is getting in full swing. Salt causes one's body to hold fluids. The second Chakra is primarily fed with fluids and is our emotional center where our feelings become known in the body.

The salt causes the body to hold onto the energy quality of the Chakra. One could imagine this is symbolic of attempting to either suppress or control the emotions stimulated by the stress of friends and family prevalent in this Season. Noticing this connection can give you the understanding to slow down, and lovingly accept these interactions. This will shift your pre-occupation with this one area in your body, and help the energy flow more evenly through all Chakras. Once this mental shift has occurred, your craving for salt will disappear.

Energy Circulation

An energy current, or flow of energy, exists in the body. Today's medical science recognizes the polarity of the brain. The left side deals in logical reason, objectivity, measurable ideas; the right side perceives things in a much more freeform way. The left side of the brain does logical tasks such as writing software or clinical experiments, and is associated with masculine characteristics. Greatest activity occurs in the right side of the brain when doing such tasks as writing a poem or painting a picture, and is associated with our feminine aspect.

The left side of the body is controlled by the right side of the brain, representing the feminine part of our duality (receptive, *taking in*). The right side of our bodies is controlled by the left side of the brain, and represents our masculine aspect *(putting out)*. These aspects of our physical form create a circulation of energy.

Your left hand and foot pull in energy that then circulates toward the center of the body. Your right hand and foot put out energy. It strikes me as odd that we shake hands with our right hands. Both actors' energies flow outward meeting in the clasped hands.

Have you ever seen someone extend their left hand and place it on top of the two right hands shaking? It is a very friendly and sincere gesture. The reason it seems this way is it serves to offer a receptive release line into which the energy buildup of the two right hands shaking can be released. It brings a balance that eases any tension.

A much more natural way to greet someone is holding out both hands, taking their hands in ours: our right to their left, their right to our left. This creates an energy vortex as the energy flows down right arms and is received by the left. Looking down from overhead, the energy would naturally flow counterclockwise through both bodies. As the energy freely circulates between the two individuals, it gives them a full experience and appreciation of each other. This creates a warm open encounter between two actors.

To feel this energy flow, and prove its existence to the doubting left side of your brain, get together with several friends. Stand in a circle facing inward and hold hands. As everyone extends their hands to one another, hold your hands "thumbs left" so the connection will be consistent around the circle. This will serve to maximize the flow of energy. Then just stand together. You can say a poem together, or sing a song, or say a chant, or simply concentrate on sending your energy out your right hand.

After a short while you will begin to feel the energy coming in your left hand and going out your right. It will feel like a throb, or a tingle, or a tickling sensation. If someone in the circle is not receptive to this experiment, they can actually shut down their conductivity, and the flow of the energy will be retarded.

When holding an object to feel its energy, or when drawing cards during divination playtime, use your left hand so you are more receptive to the possibilities. Using your right hand introduces your own energy as it flows naturally out from the body, and may color your experience.

Another natural energy flow in the body involves the chakras. Although energy pulses in and out rapidly in the chakras, each has a predominant direction in which energy flows through it.

7th, crown chakra	Out
6th, third eye chakra	In
5th, throat chakra	Out
4th, heart chakra	In
3rd, solar plexus chakra	Out
2nd, sacral chakra	In
1st, base chakra	Out

As you review the basic qualities of each chakra, you may see a correlation between the Out (masculine) and In (feminine) aspects of each. A snakelike energy line is formed by this in and out pattern, flowing from Base to Crown. This serpent-like undulation is the line on which kundalini energy can be experienced in the body.

Changes Ahead

What I have generally described has been the form of our human instrument for some time now. However, with the new loving energies and higher vibration coming into our planet, there is information coming in about our changing form.

As time goes by, our scientific community will validate more of this. We will hear about changes in our DNA strands, shifts in our magnetic North pole affecting our bodies' polarities, a transition from a more dense form to a higher frequency Light body. *These times, they are a-changin'.*

On my Nordic Track tour through the chakra centers of my body, an unscheduled stop between my 3rd and 4th chakras has become more persistent. This new chakra has a lime or yellow-green color.

One morning, I saw yellow and green diagonal stripes when I looked down upon this new front chakra. As the chakra turned, it appeared like an old-fashion barber pole sign, moving like a corkscrew. Then I saw a ring encompassing the chakra that moved away from the body and back again crisply, similar to the movement of a manual credit card imprinter being worked. As the ring passed over the yellow and green stripes, they merged into the lime green of its usual appearance.

I call this new friend my diaphragmatic center, because it is strongly connected with the movement of breath in and out of the lungs. Yet it is not as much involved with the exchange of oxygen and carbon dioxide, as it is with a general exchange of energy flowing in and out of my body. It is as if it helps with the assimilation of the coarser energy from below into the higher frequencies of those chakras above.

These sensations within our Beings are most exciting. Many of us are intrigued with the vision of attaining our Light body, and moving into a condition of Ascension while still in physical form. Ridged templates of how things have been, are beginning to dissolve in the evidence of new ways flowing into our experience. Is that tingling between my shoulder blades truly the start of my evolving Light body's wings, growing as I open to the possibility?

*Dear Divine Oneness, may I remain open during this time
of transition, allowing room for all that might be, while
keeping my mind free from comfortable, established beliefs.
Let me soar into the future with courage and confidence.*

Health Adventures

As you travel through your life, you will write experiences
into your script having to do with the health of your body.
These events allow your deeper understanding to come forward. Although you are a spiritual Being, you are here so you
can experience events through the sensory equipment in your
body. Befriending and appreciating your amazing physical form
can do much to enhance your receptivity to personal growth.

Going to the doctor is a ritual in which many participate. If
you are sensing something out-of-balance in your system, it can
be helpful to get opinions from an outside source. Of course,
the broken bone can definitely benefit from the physician's
educated attention.

In a less extreme instance, a doctor can help you gain a clear
understanding of what area in your body is being affected. This
can help you know what to address, so the true causes underlying the condition can be resolved. These opinions you receive
serve as useful information. However, never forget to test the
accuracy of their words by how they feel as they strike your
ears and heart.

Remember to always expect the unexpected. There is always
a possibility that the most important reason you go to the
doctor is a magazine article you read in the waiting room! Do
not use your weakened physical state as an excuse to fall into

automatic behavior. Retain your conscious awareness no matter how common place the situation.

When you require a doctor's assistance, the demeanor of the doctor you consult will very much reflect the clarity of your intent to become well. If you duck your responsibility, figure the physician is wiser in knowledge about your body's welfare, and you give your power away, you will find yourself facing an insensitive egotist who barely takes time to talk to you. If you go into the exchange as an equal with the physician, ready to help find what is wrong, you will find just the opposite is true.

If you work from a responsible position regarding your health, you will put illnesses behind you more quickly. After all, the whole incident is something you wrote into your script for yourself. A long term dis-ease or distress will stay with you until you have understood and accepted the growth it has come to facilitate.

Many alternative health professionals consciously work in concert with the natural process of the body. They understand that they do not hold the power to heal you. They are facilitators, who maximize the potential for your health to return to you. Focusing their love, from their own God-connection, they promote the resolution of any outstanding lesson issues in your script. This creates a broader base from which to approach a healing.

Medical science is beginning to recognize the affect love and touch has on promoting wellness. Meditation is also being taught as a tress reducer, and as a way to uplift one's frame of mind. Resistance in the medical community to use these more subtle treatment forms will continue to lessen. The truth of the results encourages their use.

We are each a unique Being, and our body's needs reflect this. For example, each body's requirements to sustain and nourish itself will vary a bit. Each of us requires varying amounts of different nutrients. Each actor will react to such things as exposure to the sun, allergens, prescription drugs, etc. in their own way.

Our physical predisposition was designed to best serve our story line. These tendencies were carefully crafted into our body while it formed within our mothers. If a particular heredity characteristic best serves the actor, this is a consideration in the selection of the parents before conception.

The natural state of the physical body is to retain the form provided in our prenatal template. Unless particular defects have been fashioned into your form to serve a theme in your script, this base state is a condition of health and wholeness. If you are primarily well in this lifetime, this will be your natural condition.

Catching a cold or flu, or even breaking a bone, are experiences we choose for our growth. Often our body is requesting nothing more than we slow a bit and rest.

As you move more in harmony with your natural script's flow, you will find fewer incidences of the annual illnesses that plague our world. You will learn to know when your body needs a break. You can take some time out, without your body having to force the issue by catching a cold or flu.

Within the body, each of our organs and structural components has its unique signature vibration. In Nature, plants and flowers exist that share similar frequencies. These compatible vibrations from Nature, can be brought into one's system in such forms as tinctures or aromatic oils, to assist the dis-eased body in returning to its healthy, whole condition.

There are even devices being invented, similar to ultrasound, which can bombard an area in the body with the frequency equal to its healthy state. When we are unwell, the frequency of some portion of our body has gotten off-key, and it has forgotten its perfect pitch. By artificially introducing the correct frequency, the body can be helped to recall its cellular memory of health.

At a cellular level, we carry the knowledge of what the healthy condition is like in every part of our body. In truth, our body does not know how to be anything other than healthy. Becoming well is nothing more than returning to our natural state. If we are ready—at our soul's level—to be well, it is a most natural process to resolve an illness, to remember and return to wholeness.

Be sensitive to the sources you choose when getting herbs, vitamin and mineral supplement, and the like. Products prepared with care and love will offer the most beneficial vibration to your Being. Only use those things to which you find yourself naturally attracted. This is not a good area to rely solely on another person's recommendations, unless you know each other well, and feel comfortable that your opinions are in harmony. Your body has a good idea what it needs. Listen to its subtle instructions.

Water

Fluids are of utmost importance to our bodies, and Water heads the list. All other fluids require that the body separate water from the other ingredients. This additional processing of liquids causes a sense of stress in the body. Water is what our bodies need.

I always enjoyed a particular episode on the original Star Trek television series. They encountered an alien species whose physical form varied greatly from ours. These aliens referred to humans as, "ugly bags of mostly water." That's us! We must forgive their judgment regarding the "ugly" part. Never having seen humans before, they were not able to appreciate our bipedal beauty. Perspectives are very personal things.

Drinking a glass of water can be experienced as a deeply nurturing act. It is a love offering to our system. It provides the basic element required in the greatest quantity and frequency above all others.

Water itself is a lovely symbol of infinite transition. The hydrogen and oxygen molecules that make up our water have existed since the earliest days on our planet. Water is constantly flowing through a life cycle of falling rain, gathering into bodies of water, and finally evaporating into the clouds to fall back once again as rain. Even as humanity manages to contaminate our life-giving water sources, our planet and her cycles work miracles to filter out a great deal of the damage done. Without water, our bodies die, and far more quickly than without food.

Next time you are fortunate enough to pour a glass of water from a faucet in your home, pause and realize what you are doing. Its simple appearance belies its ancient past of adventure, as it traveled through and around our planet. Thank dear Mother Earth for freely offering her bounties. Look upon this timeless nectar that has flowed on our planet for millions of years. Lift it to your lips as you would toast your Beingness with a fine champagne. Bless and thank your body for its tireless service, as you lovingly introduce this pure fluid of life. Feel the water move down your throat and into your stomach. Allow yourself to fully feel this physical miracle of your body that carries your spiritual soul through your script. Know in this simple act of drinking water that you are celebrating your Body and your Self.

Our miraculous body connects our spiritual essence into all of the wonders that make up our physical world. It links us subtly, and completely, into the energy web that is the Whole of Creation, which includes the spirit realm. It allows us the vehicle through which so much growth can occur. What a priceless gift from God, our higher-self and our parents.

Celebrate your body in your movements, your sensuous experience of the world's colors, textures, sounds, tastes and scents carried on the air. Seek its advice so you might feed it what it needs. Feel its joyful involvement as you swim or cycle, walk, jog, hike, or simply use your muscles in your normal activities that fill each day.

Thank your wonderful mind for allowing you the ability to know your consciousness, while in this physical form. Embrace and love the bone and muscle, organs, glands, circulatory system, and glorious features and hair that give our exterior its unique quality. Our body truly is the actor's instrument.

Tell Me How To Create The Life I Want

YOUR LIFE IS YOUR CREATION. Each actor has a personal approach that makes his life unique among all others. Even if one attempts to copy the antics of someone they admire, the similarities will be shallow. Every one of us has no choice but to lead our own lives, wherever that may take us. The knack is to learn how you can craft your life, into that which your imagination desires.

Personal Creation

All human creations start in the mind. Imagine a shape, your shape. Draw a picture of your shape. Go to a store (home remodeling, hobby supply, etc.) and find some material out of which you can construct or mold your shape. Once completed, look at it. Understand that what you can now hold in your hands, and rest your eyes upon, would not exist if you had not created it from your imagination.

If ideas come up and will not leave you alone, they are looking for expression. If your heart is involved as the idea frolics through your mind, you may as well get used to the thought. Eventually it will want your complete personal attention.

Even during the process of moving the flickering idea into a physical expression, it may lead you through an evolution of ideas and experiences. The final product can be quite different in detail from what was first imagined. Hold your ideas gently to leave room for the infinite possibilities at work to refine them.

Your frame of mind in each moment is also your creation. It is the quality of your frame of mind that creates a chord, which colors the events in your life. You absolutely create the flavor of your own experiences. You even create your perspective, from which you evaluate these events.

Recognize what you want in your life, and feel yourself moving into this scene in your imagination. In your most active times of change, relating to other actors can disrupt your concentration on where you are going. Seek the company of those who support you in your desires. Avoid those who resist your desire for change. If you are sincere and clear on your direction, you will find your own style of getting there. You have all the guidance nearby that you need.

Realize you fully deserve that which you desire. You can use your natural power to create it for yourself. Reviewing a thought silently has a creative power in it. Expressing the thought aloud, brings even more of your energy to bear, moving the thought more quickly into your reality. Finally, writing the words down, speaking them aloud, and then handling the document with respect, yields the highest level of creative energy.

You can move your desire from a single-engine airplane, to a supersonic jet.

Here is a tangible example of personal creation. While standing on a street corner with traffic moving by, it may be your desire to cross the street. You must solicit the cooperation of those actors in the big metal things on wheels, in order for your desire to manifest. If you stand quietly with your back to the oncoming cars, it could be a very long time before an opening in traffic might present itself.

Instead, make eye contact with your fellow actors. Move strongly to the edge of the crosswalk with full expectation of crossing the street. Drivers in the cars will respond to your actions. They will take notice. Your *intent* to cross their busy road becomes known to them.

If they are functioning in cooperation with the community of actors on Stage, they find reason to honor your desire. They pull in their several hundred horses, and pause for your desire to be fulfilled. Of course, there might also be those actors firmly within their ego's control, who savor the opportunity to show their undeniable power. I would not quite step off the curb until the true color of those in the immediate area was evaluated. It does not take much to know their intent, if you look for it.

You can create your wishes on more subtle levels as well. If you are having difficulties in a relationship or situation, you can look above it, and create an opportunity for improvement. Every actor has an angelic higher-self with whom they can communicate. These Beings exist in the full knowledge of God's Love and Divine Wholeness.

There is a lovely technique described in *The Dynamic Laws of Healing*, by Catherine Ponder. You can *write a letter to the angel* of the actor with whom you are having difficulty. Write this letter in positive terms, asking that your experiences with this person become free from restrictions. Describe and affirm the positive situation you would like to create.

As with any time you consciously address the Universe, use clear loving positive words. Use as few words as possible, while still making your request clear. Once complete, place the letter somewhere safe and private. It is for the angel's and your eyes-only; the secrecy keeps the intent pure and uninterrupted. Then, allow some time for results. This can be a surprisingly powerful way to clear difficulties and delays from the situation.

Discernment

Understanding you have a powerful ability to create what you desire, merely gives you the tools needed. It is your decisions around what you wish to create that gives your life shape and definition.

To know clearly what you want, you must first be an observer of your natural Self. You must come into synch with your soul's purpose. To come to this place of cooperative existence with the Self takes great discernment.

Remember, most of us have spent our entire lives responding to the scene we are living by using methods taught by mothers, fathers, friends, and teachers. It is rare for these people of influence to have had spiritually wise instruction within their own scripts. Therefore it may be difficult for them to look beneath the surface of events. So the techniques you have been given by these actors, only serve ego-level behavior. These limited guide-lines only open to three-dimensional possibilities, instead of the multidimensional possibilities an enlightened human has at their disposal.

You wrote your script's outline broadly, leaving room for improvisation and inspiration. Consciously embrace your adventure. Respond to what you see occurring in your life by considering the meaning, or symbology, of what is happening.

Issues prior to, and beyond, this physical life influence the dialogue and scope of our experiences. They come from cur-rents and desires that flow through many lifetimes. How they surface for review and action in a specific moment, has a tremendous history flowing with it.

Our perspective, on how past lifetimes affect our current lifetime, might be likened to what happens in Nature. If a large tree is killed back by frost, it can be cut down to the ground to promote fresh growth: a rebirth. The small new green Being that appears gives the impression of a new tree, yet it has an adult root ball pushing its growth. Everyone viewing the young tree will consider it far from experienced in the world. Yet what appears young, has the wisdom of the adult tree guiding it to its full-grown manifestation.

We have bounties of experience and knowledge, just below the conscious surface, ready to help us move effortlessly through the years. Allow this information to flow up from inside—from your roots—and the broader understanding of what is going on in your life will become more clear.

Often we are presented with what appears to be an obstacle. If it pops up unexpectedly in front of us, it is likely an illusion of someone else's creation. If we accept the obstacle as real, we give it our energy, and create it for ourselves. Instead, recognize it as an illusion and ignore it. Its impact on our life will be severely minimized. If you have ever ignored a perceived problem, and found it resolving itself, you have experienced the situation I am describing.

If you find yourself reacting strongly to something that is being said or done, you have just received a wonderful gift of self-discovery. Shift your focus from the external situation causing your reaction, to why your reaction has come to your attention. You may find it is presenting an aspect of yourself that you do not like. The experience may give you enough knowledge of its existence, within yourself, to allow you to forgive it and release it from your expression.

Another possibility is that you may be witnessing a scene showing an expression of a quality within yourself that you have meant to investigate, but have not yet made time. The scene, being played out before you, may be a poor imitation of the higher expression of which you know yourself capable. It may show you that even at the weakest level of expression, this quality is still of value to those in the scene. This may give you the courage and confidence you lacked previously, to take up the challenge. The experience can become the catalyst that gets you active in this new direction.

Your strong reaction could also be a breakthrough in remembering a hurt, or wound, from a previous lifetime. It allows you the opportunity to seek it out, and release it. Whatever the case, if your reaction is out of proportion to the current meaning of the scene unfolding, look deeper for your personal message involved.

As you begin to recognize disruptions in your life as valuable nuggets of self-knowledge, they will bother you less. You will begin to sense the deeper levels of energy currents, flowing in your life. You will begin to understand how to move with these currents, so that you work with them, instead of offering resistance. Working in this way brings you into synch with the natural you.

Others will try to control and manipulate you, by giving you orders or laying down laws that they require you follow. Their story line is testing the limits of their ego's power. However, whether they succeed in their control depends on whether you cooperate or not. One person cannot have an argument; an argument requires two participants. If someone chooses to spend precious time creating judgments of you, it is their choice affecting only them. It is only yourself you need to please.

The more you open to your natural direction, the more evident your direction will become. It is far easier to live the life you designed in your production meeting, before the curtain went up. It is "the sweet spot of your contract," as Kryon of Lee Carroll's books would say. The contract you made with yourself. It is where you meant yourself to be. The place where each potential you possess flows gently into being.

Everyone, all actors, all Plays, are moving in an exquisitely complex and beautiful dance with one another. We are all inseparably interconnected within the vibration that is the Whole of Creation. This Oneness, which we mistakenly view as an infinite bunch of pieces, is more accurately a weaving of all things into a single rich tapestry. Using our gift of free will, we make choices in each moment, which affect the direction in which we move through our local environment, dear Mother Earth.

Employment

Most actors choose a script in which their money comes from employment for another. Once in this position, it is common practice to fall into the defensive. "If I do not behave as expected, I will lose my job." Then our ego piles on a few more fears: "My mortgage payment will be missed, we'll lose our home, we will go hungry, and end up on the street!"

In truth, an employer has a great deal of flexibility in accepting nonstandard behavior. If an employee is honestly providing the highest value performance they can, an employer cannot ask for more. The arrangement is: this person gives you some money; in exchange, you provide a service. If your heart is in honoring this commitment, your employer will recognize your efforts.

Now if your heart is not in it, you are in the wrong place. Start looking for an employer who moves in harmony with your own energy. Find a vision behind which you can throw your 100% participation. Ask all of your questions before accepting employment. Walk through the place of employment while everyone is working, and open your pores. You can read a lot between the lines from the energy drifting through the hallways.

If your boss demands certain behavior, do not follow his lead unless you are in agreement. Testing all instructions against your body's sensations is how you know if something is in synch with the real you. Without full agreement on your part, you are not being true to yourself. This seemingly self-absorbed attitude, or self-interest, is *very* important.

From another's perspective, such discerning behavior may make you appear detached, stubborn, selfish, or foolish. This is their perception. It does not affect you. If you do feel their criticisms, understand you are operating from your worldly-ego's perspective. When this happens, simply notice what you are doing, and let it go. You will feel your concern over their judgments melt into nothingness.

If you have managed to get yourself hired somewhere that the energy and direction do not match your own, you are there for a definite reason. There are no mistakes. You would not have written it into your script if it did not present hidden value. You may be there to finally learn your lesson, and break your pattern around sublimating your own desires to those with which you do not agree. You may be ready to proclaim your personal freedom from such influences. Or perhaps those people making up the business organization are ready to shift their direction, and you are there to serve as the catalyst. There may be others there that are equally distressed by the circumstances. They may find the courage, from your example, to make the choice to follow their own hearts and true being.

Once you know you can no longer agree with the directions given by your employer, the choice after that becomes much clearer. If you succumb to the pressure and backslide, forgive yourself and regroup.

Each choice is a fresh chance to sing the song of your own heart. Whether you choose to break from the group loudly, making your discord perfectly clear, or more quietly, keeping a low profile, your choice to follow only what is in accord with yourself will have its effect on those around you.

Once you have found the employer that warms your heart, simply pay attention. When someone asks you to do something, make sure it makes sense to you. You cannot do a task lovingly from the heart, if you are acting mechanically from the mind.

Once you understand the task assigned, be sure to question whether there might be a better way to do it. If you willingly participate in a business, new ways of approaching old tasks will pop into your mind. There will be no begrudging feelings blocking your natural creative flow. You will become a guide to others who function fearfully in the same environment. You can help others by showing how to work within prescribed boundaries while being yourself.

If you are approaching your work with this open attitude, the value of your efforts will be fair exchange for the moneys received. Even the number of hours you work ought to balance out with your life. Most employers will give you more and more to do. You have two choices: (1) accept the increasing tasks without objection, or (2) tell your employer when there is not enough of you to go around. *Championing the quality of your life is in your hands.*

If you work longer hours to accomplish your assignments, the balance will go out of your life. Once you have pushed yourself beyond your ability to remain balanced, the quality of attention you have available, for every moment of each day, will decline. You will lose your sensitivity to knowing the subtle messages from your true Self. You cannot replace quality with quantity without expecting to pay a high price.

So when you have reached your maximum load, choose (2) above and explain: the new task can be done, but something else must slip. Suffering in silence does no one any good. If someone tells you all things must be done yesterday, it becomes your assignment to rethink your choice of employers.

NOTHING is more important than retaining your natural balance. If you are exhausted all the time, the real purpose of your life will never have a chance to dance in the consciousness of your Being. You will walk through life asleep, missing your subtle crossroads of opportunity.

It is your divine oath to yourself, as the hero of your Play, to move through your life in accord with your true higher-self. Your heart and mind are of highest value when they help you understand how each choice—for example, whether to follow your boss's orders—matches what feels right to you.

When Things Go Wrong

Life is meant to be fun, with everything flowing smoothly and easily. However, it is not always so.

Each of us can wake up into a dark day. Our lightness of heart is missing, and instead, a heaviness exists. Our way seems anything but clear. Expending effort seems all but impossible. What to do next is not apparent. Everyone around us seems energetic and moving forward with purpose. They do little more than provide a sad comparison to highlight how far off track our Being has strayed. Once stalled so, at the edge of despair, it seems beyond imagination that we will ever move forward confidently again...

When you find yourself at such a place (and everyone will), do not slip into automatic behavior, and suppress your true condition from yourself. Part of your new agreement with yourself is to love you unconditionally—for better or for worse—and to stand in full awareness of your Being and condition.

What you are experiencing is for a reason. Allow yourself to look at it head on, and feel its affect at every level of your Being. Have compassion for yourself as you would for any soul in the midst of a trying time.

One morning, I awoke after a night of tossing and turning. I reviewed the dream that was drifting swiftly out of reach. The dream events that I recalled were filled with people too busy to pay me the attention I needed. I was unable to complete whatever my task was in the dream. I had the heavy taste of "poor me, poor me" on my mind.

I had been struggling with this book in recent days. What to be written next was not apparent. I had been consulting my pendulum to answer the percentage of completion of each chapter. It seemed even my pendulum had little interest in the questions, as its swing was slight rather than strong and answers came slowly.

As I started my day and moved into my room to meditate, the full depth of my depression came heavily to rest on my shoulders. As I sat in my dark green wingback chair, I reached for my deck of Angel Cards in their turquoise pouch. As I held them gently between my cupped hands, I closed my eyes and said the words that came up in my mind.

> *"Dear Friends, what words are most appropriate for me*
> *on this day? What words will reach past the darkness in*
> *which I find myself, to gently point my way? What words*
> *will buoy up my spirit, allowing the highest expression of*
> *my true Being to naturally flow through? What words are*
> *most appropriate for me on this day?"*

Then reaching into the pouch I drew three cards as was usual, and then a fourth as I was compelled to do. The words COMPASSION, WILLINGNESS, HONESTY and TRUST lay before me. I gazed at the colorful angelic illustrations and handsome calligraphy on each card, and asked.

> *"Dear guides and Spirit, help me understand the meaning*
> *in these cards so the Highest Good may be done."*

COMPASSION: Looking at the first word, I felt the loving presence surrounding me. But in this instance I understood this card meant having compassion for myself. I needed to gently handle my Being during such times of sadness, to accept myself no matter how I felt or behaved. I also needed to forgive myself instead of critically finding fault.

WILLINGNESS: I understood the importance of being willing to feel, and be, where I found myself. Only this would allow all that could be learned from the experience to have opportunity to come forward.

HONESTY: I needed to be honest with myself. I was—if even for the moment—totally lost. I needed to seek beyond my own Being for guidance, from the Source.

TRUST: And no matter how lost I might feel, I needed to trust in God, and the process of living. By consciously moving through my life with gentle and thorough awareness, the dynamic occurrences would guide me in every moment.

Suddenly, a more specific personal message jelled in my mind. I had forgotten the simplest thing. In looking (so hard) for the next thing to write in this book, *I had forgotten to let the material flow naturally from the events unfolding in my life.* In that moment, I understood how important it was for me to have come to a total impasse. I had to remember what had been forgotten.

Where I stood, within that moment, was a place most actors have visited. Although the specifics of each actor's predicament will vary widely, that sense of being caught with one's hand in the cookie jar, makes the moment of resolution common to all.

As the full understanding, and acceptance, of the moment washed over me like a surging river, I saw the breaking Light before me. A discernible shift clicked into place.

Later as I drove to work, dear Mother Earth offered up scenes more beautiful than I ever believed could have been conjured! The songs of birds were profuse, and especially sweet and varied. Once in my car, I started one of Rusty Crutcher's Sacred Site Series audiotapes I had not heard before. The clear melodic tones and digitally recorded sounds of Nature caressed my soul.

It was as if I was alone on the highway, as traffic opened before me at every turn. As I crossed the Bayside Bridge and looked across the still water to Tampa in the distance, I could not believe the beauty before me. A broad towering thunderhead stood out white and billowy against the deep blue morning sky. The sun was just hidden below its rim, making its edges a brilliant silver-white. I could barely look upon the brightness.

Far below at the waterline, the depth of the thundercloud brought a darkness streaked with diagonal lines as heavy rain was blown by the distant winds. The contrast and immensity of the scene struck my senses into a thousand strands of attention that drank in the sight as the moment stood still. The bounties of the beautiful Earth were showering Blessings in confirmation that I had indeed understood the message that morning. The darkness in my core was shattered and dissolved, carried ever away on wings beating only into a distant memory.

I was fortunate that I had listened openly to the synthesis of energy in the combined meanings of the words presented. I had asked for help, received, and accepted the information synthesized that morning. As the days moved on, I found abundant material flowing forth again from happenings in my life. I was no longer concerned for which chapter it was meant. I was simply satisfied that Spirit focused my attention on a seed thought that would flower forth into many paragraphs.

No matter how enlightened or balanced an actor becomes, there are times when our forward momentum can be stalled by a sadness, human confusion, or even something hidden, like lesson material still due to be experienced. We are in human form. The guidance descending into us from our higher-self and Spirit is not always clear.

When you are in need of clarification and assistance, ask for it. You can never be denied your answer when you request it with true intent. What you need be aware of is: it may not always be the answer you want!

Handling Guilt

Know life is meant to be fluid and easy. Watch for times when you are caught up in emotional situations, which slow your way. Remember that these things cannot affect your progress unless you share your consciousness with them. Forgive yourself, the other actor(s), the situation, and let go of this emotional baggage.

Guilt can be particularly troublesome. Like other negative parasites, guilt only has a foothold if you allow it. If someone expects you to come to Thanksgiving dinner, but your script has other plans for that day, there is no need to feel sorry. If you allow yourself to be emotionally blackmailed into doing things that run contrary to the natural course of your life, you are not placing your priorities where they were meant to be.

Sadly, you cannot directly affect another actor's perspective of your choices. All you can do is: love them for who they are, and let it go. If you succumb to their pressure, and feel guilty, you are creating emotional IOUs that will be carried forward with you. This is not part of the natural process of living. It keeps you from freely getting on with your own life.

FORGIVE YOURSELF for not being able to satisfy everyone in every moment. Understand it is with yourself that you must move in accord. If others truly love you, they will honor your desires. If you mean no harm by your decisions, then *no real harm can be done.* The purity of your intention is always known, even if the other person does not want to admit it. If the other person chooses to feel hurt by your decision, it is up to you to resist playing into their game.

Relationships are a prime area where guilt can run amuck. We can learn at a very young age that assigning guilt is an effective tool in influencing others, so that we get our own way. We can also recognize its value when practiced upon *ourselves*, to alter our own behavior to avoid dealing with some scary, imagined thing.

Guilt is the most efficient tool for manipulating actors that exists in physicality. However, on today's scorecard of life, none of us owe each other anything. Therefore no real basis exists on which this imagined imbalance can sustain itself, without your help.

It is appropriate that we freely give honor and respect to one another. It is appropriate to give thanks to your parents, for the wonderful body they willingly formed in your honor. At this point, all imagined obligations have been satisfied.

Everyone knew basically what would happen in your relationships, and agreed to the script before your Play commenced. If an extremely intense incident appears in your life, it may be a karmic repayment at work. Even this can be recognized, and resolved, without the level of suffering that is often seen.

Guilt is laced with a silent threat of love withheld. However, **you do not have to do anything special to earn love.** By the mere fact of your unique God-spark Beingness, you always deserve and are given unconditional love. There are no rules around this. Do not let other actors *or yourself* tell you otherwise. You will find that the lack of being loved is an attribute of your own perspective. You must practice your ability to receive the Love being shone upon you.

If you feel guilty, you cannot be free of it by simply dismissing it, and pushing it down into your subconscious. Your feelings are real things. Your body stores them as cellular memories. You must look inside, and pull this guilt out, into the light of your focused attention. You must forgive yourself for having allowed this manipulative "thing" to grab hold of you.

See any guilt for what it is. There is no love or caring in it, only hopes to manipulate your choices. Tell it there is no longer room for it in yourself. Hold your hands cupped before you, and *feel* the guilt trickling out of yourself and into your hands. *FEEL IT EXITING YOUR BODY.*

When it is all held within your hands, tell it you are setting it free, dissolving its need to be. Say you forgive yourself for receiving this guilt, and the person or situation for providing it. Then, as if you had a beautiful white dove nestled there, lift your hands quickly upwards and apart, releasing this heavy emotional stuff to scatter into the ethers. Feel its departure. Feel the sense of freedom in its place. *Feel it being gone!*

Allow yourself the gift of freeing yourself from these weighty issues. You deserve a light load on your journey.

Group Dynamics

Although we are truthfully alone in the midst of the sifting sands of our Play, often we experience events as one of many actors involved. Interacting effectively in a group, while maintaining our personal balance as a unique Being, takes keen awareness.

Strong ego personalities can take charge in a group, pulling the focus out of the individual's hands. However, for a group to be taken over by a single individual, the others have to give their power willingly. No one can control you unless you allow it. It is (as always) your choice.

One morning as I drove to work, a school bus stopped my progress in the subdivision where I lived. I had often seen a bus picking up children at this intersection. This was where parents and small elementary-school-aged children congregated each morning to wait for the bus. This morning scene had always given the impression of quite a social gathering, with much smiling, talking, gesturing of hands, and sloshing of coffee cups.

This morning, something was different. The bus faced in the opposite direction than was usual. I nodded my head in agreement as I heard my guides say "New driver." What was usually a one or two minute delay was showing no sign of ending. Mothers were chatting to the driver through the window of the bus, and other child drop-off vehicles blocked my passage.

One mother, recognizing I was unable to pass, approached the sport utility vehicle parked at the curb, requesting they move to let me by. I could only gather from the vehicle's non-movement that her request met with resistance. I silently honored her for working from a perspective outside the group's mind set.

Finally I climbed out of my car and approached the bus driver's window. "What's going on?" I asked. The new driver explained she was several minutes ahead of the posted pickup time, and she planned to wait until then to depart. Then she asked "Would you like me to move the bus so you can get by?" "Thank you, I would like to get to work," and I was walking back to my car. What happened next was subtle, but unmistakable.

Many parents were looking at me with anger in their faces! I could not believe their reaction to my simple request. I smiled at their expressions and body language.

As the bus pulled to the side and I drove by, a father was motioning vehemently at me as he drew a circle in the air. He was angrily mouthing "Go around, go around!" showing I could have reversed my direction and traveled other streets to get by without disturbing the bus. This only served to make me smile more broadly.

What had happened? I had dared to interrupt their group's scene, steeped in the tradition from many mornings together. The energy that I encountered struck me as similar to that of an angry street gang. Somehow I had offended them, and had brought out their wrath.

If I had been walking down a narrow hallway, and a single individual had blocked my way, a request for passage would have been honored without a moment's hesitation, and without anger at having been asked. The bus driver was not upset. She knew being off schedule was not enough reason to block traffic on a public highway. She moved her bus without a second thought. However, the adults on foot, gripped by the group's mob-mentality, had found this an affront.

Every morning at this street intersection, all of the various actors come together, proudly shepherding their sweet youngsters. As they arrive at this place, the energy of the corner takes on a distinct sense. They are all proud of their parental caring, and solid in their righteous task of keeping watch, until their children are safely driven away in the bus. I had often noted the aura of important purpose as I drove this way each morning. At other times during the day, this place is simply an intersection, like so many others.

What happens when people get together to form a group, joined in a purpose, is most amazing. If each actor is operating from knowledge of their personal responsibility in their life, then exciting dynamic exchanges can occur. In its most positive form, each member of the group retains their unique individual voice, while sharing and creating group ideas.

If one interrupts such a gathering, one finds each individual working independently of a group mind. The interruption is handled much like passing the single individual in the hallway mentioned earlier. The group of individuals resolves what is needed, and without one bit of wasted energy or attention, they shift back to continue from where the interruption occurred.

What I experienced was much different. The group of parents had lost their individual stance. They had become focused into one mind. As such, they were operating from a reality base that overreacted with hostility. Because they were many, and I was one, they were shocked and upset that I would have put my personal desire above maintaining the status quo of their scene.

Even a group setting is made up of individuals. We are many actors, independently living our lives. Each individual actor is due honor and respect for their purpose of being. No one person is more important, or better, than another. Each actor is equal in the eyes of God.

Be aware as you interact with groups of actors. It can be easy to drop into automatic, and meld into the group mind. You release your personal responsibility and flow mindlessly with what happens. This is how actors were able to say, "I was only following orders..." when they helped take the several million lives during Hitler's reign in the Second World War.

Whether it feels this way or not, you are always functioning as an individual. As this powerfully focused expression of energy, be discerning about whom you join. Every moment, make sure you are with energy that truly agrees with you from the heart. Do not settle for anything else.

Life Dynamics

You make progress in moving your life toward what you would prefer when you focus on yourself, by yourself. You change the world around you, by first changing your world within.

Your energy changes when you change your internal point-of-view. Once changed, the Universe goes into motion to equalize your energy with that surrounding you. Likes attract Likes. Things and people whose energy is unlike yours move away.

It is the internal change that causes the changes in your environment, your friends, your relationships, etc. Your outer life will suggest those energies that are in harmony with your inner self.

Similarly, if you willfully put yourself into places that run contrary to your natural energy, your internal system will

attempt to shift into agreement with the external. If you are
among positive influences, your vibration will be increased.
If you choose to be in lower vibratory surroundings, your
vibration can be pulled lower. This begins to limit your ability
to fulfill your potentials.

Some actors enjoy making large changes often. The swirl
of energies released brings a great deal of action into their lives.
They feed off this sense of excitement, and yearn for more.
A tranquil life would bore them to tears: one actor's preference.
Whatever their style, the Divine embraces all actors equally,
with love and compassion.

Once when in my early twenties, I had a boy friend with
whom I felt a bit uneasy. To all external appearances, he seemed
kind and easy going. We enjoyed outdoor activities, and developed many friends in common in our outings. He never did
anything directly that would account for the way my internal
voice was warning me.

One afternoon, we were hanging out at his home, doing
nothing in particular. Suddenly I stood up, excused myself, and
left. I felt so compelled to do so that I did not question this
almost involuntary action. I never spent another minute with
him. Our relationship was over.

I had never severed a relationship so completely in such an
abrupt manner. Strangely, it surprised both of us. All I can
imagine is the energy between us was in disharmony. My energy
was not changing, nor was his. The moment arrived when my
internal state could no longer deal with the imbalance. My will
to remain in his presence was overruled by the common sense

of the Universe. My physical body simply picked up and delivered itself elsewhere, out of his influence.

Our Play is one continuous fluid event, from the moment of birth, to the moment of our physical death. Although it is difficult to refrain from perceiving life as a jumble of this and that, all tossed together, there is a continuity and purpose that cements our life vignettes together.

Our choices in every moment create the script that spreads before us as we journey. The wonders and situations that appear, attracted by our growth's requirements, provide the rich environment in which we Play our way to our tomorrow.

We write close associations into our scripts for mutual growth. Whether it is a spouse, children, or an alliance with friends of similar a mindset, there will be a rich opportunity for interactions.

If you are with supportive loving people, you will feel stimulated and enlivened. However, if you participate in negative interpersonal games, you will feel sad and empty. As with employers, you have choices with whom you affiliate. If you are honest with yourself and others, your choices will be for the best of all concerned.

If someone says something that hurts you, it is your **choice** to feel hurt that allows the pain. No one has true control over you. It is your life's script. The pen is in your hand.

One grows to *know* that it is in the Divine Plan for the Universe to support our desires and intentions that are free from ego contamination. When we agree to live in harmony, and in the highest good for all living things, our way is paved with rose pedals. We will not starve to death, or go without shelter, unless these are experiences we have purposefully written into our Play's script.

There are two distinct activities you can use that together continually improve the quality of your life. The first is to actively work at perfecting your creative abilities to **bring into your life** those elements your imagination and guidance suggests.

Equally important is identifying, then forgiving and **releasing,** aspects in your life that you would prefer were gone. Sometimes it takes a while to recognize what these inharmonious elements are. They may be so ingrained that you do not recognize them as something separate from the *real You*: the spiritual nugget nestled within your core.

Along the way, angels are stationed to guide you in more areas of your life than you might imagine. Guiding angels are not only in place for individuals, but for group energies such as organizations, housing developments, cities, etc.

Through the 1980s, and well into the 1990s, my vocation was programmer/analyst. As I opened more to my guidance, I found it amusing that I had a programming angel at my side. Sometimes I would get stuck on a difficult piece of program logic, and be at a loss to solve it. I would hear a phrase of programming terms in my mind that would illuminate the solution for me. What had been beyond my mental grasp moments before, now lay clearly in the focus of my mind. "Thank you" I would say with a smile and giggle, as I began typing the revealed statements.

Even electromagnetic devices create energy that is cared for from beyond the physical. The next time your computer or telecommunication devices are giving you fits, use a few kind words and state clearly your desired resolution. You may be surprised at what happens. If the problem does not resolve itself, then look for the message this difficulty is asking you to recognize and accept.

If you choose to disregard your guidance, and willfully stomp off to do your own thing, you no longer have the depth of your natural Being underlying every action. You are making up each move from a purely ego-minded perspective. Since this mindset depends on worldly happenings on which to base its next choice of action, you no longer have natural access to the realm of Divine and infinite possibilities. Your Play becomes dull and limited in scope. You become bored, and have that hollow something-is-missing feeling in your heart. What is missing is your connection with your true Self, and your own desire to express the fullest potential of your Play.

If we listen to our egos, and try to manipulate things into going the way we would like, we meet resistance. Such mentally constructed plans limit the framework of what can happen. Even if our actions are in line with our heart's purpose, the sweetness in life will be missing. The sweetest events and feelings come when we are centered in the NOW, doing what comes naturally. It has nothing to do with the ego, or the ego's attempts to control events through the manipulation of people and things.

While you paddle your little life canoe in aimless circles, your guides, higher-self, and Divine Oneness Himself sit back with their infinitely loving patience, and wait for you to get back on track. You are never left alone. All the help ever needed is always at your side. If you open to it—talk to them in your private moments, and remain open to their subtle answers and suggestions—your life will start rolling again.

The spiritually aware actor will focus on figuring out their Play's purpose. From each moment's current understanding, all decisions are made in harmony with this purpose. The timing of each decision will naturally come when it is needed.

Procrastination is not always something to be avoided. Check with your heart. It will tell you loud and clear if you are avoiding something because you are scared or feeling lazy. However, it may simply be too early to be dealing with the issue. Those things willfully avoided through weak choices will feel like obstructions in your way. Things avoided appropriately will not influence your sensation of moving forward.

As you become more accepting of life, you will find fewer questions come up in your mind. Every actor has their own style, their own purpose, their own experience of truth and reality. Actors of every soul age are on our Planet at this time. You will not be able to understand many of the happenings that occur. The energy they represent is too different from your own.

Why does a mass murderer go on a rampage? Why do some government employees not care if they are wasting tax dollars? Why does a manufacturing firm allow their toxic waste to be dumped by unscrupulous companies to save money? None of these things are in harmony with my Play. It is not possible for me to know what is at work. There are no questions to ask. If someone is naturally drawn to one of these circumstances, it is likely the energy attracting them *is* written into their script.

Acceptance of what happens in each moment disarms your fear of what may happen in the future. The unfolding scenes in your script become warmly anticipated with excitement, instead of with dread or attempts at avoidance. You truly take your natural role as an adventurer.

Have gentle patience with yourself. Learn to let go of your habitual behavior. Move into each moment expecting fresh and new experiences. Allow yourself your birthright of imagining what you really want in this life. Allow the natural laws of the Universe to support you in your desires. Your journey may seem a crooked path, but the journey is as important as your destination. The process occurs as your life evolves, moment-by-moment.

Stay relaxed, and allow your process to carry you to your desired place. You can test your desires by how they feel in your body. If your heart smiles warmly, you need no further confirmation that your choices are valid for your script.

Stay alert as you journey. There may be things that come to your notice that will take precedence over what you felt you wanted. Always give yourself permission to re-decide what it is you want. It is your journey, your adventure.

Reunion— A Personal Story

SOMEHOW, THE KNOWLEDGE that forgiveness is a freeing experience had always been understood more in my mind than in my heart. I had always believed: if somebody crowds ahead of you in line, you just let it go; no need to be upset, right? It is not worth your time. We are always where we are meant to be, etc. So, I figured when it came to incorporating forgiveness into my life, I was in pretty good shape...

In early October 1996, I became aware of a dark oppressive energy gripping my Being. Since a tropical storm had just come through Florida, I asked some of my friends to see if they were also sensing this energy. Although everyone agreed Josephine, the storm, had weird energy, no one was feeling the same dark blanket that I was. OOPS, time to look at this from a more personal perspective.

I pulled out an astrological transit report, prepared from my Natal Chart by an experienced astrologer, to snoop into which planets and transits were influencing me. I had known for the past one and one-half years that Pluto had been opposing my

Moon. The movements of Pluto in relation to Earth had made it appear to move forwards, and then backwards in the Heavens, several times across the Natal position of my Moon. In the transit report I found Pluto, which had gone Direct again, was almost precisely opposing my moon one last time before it moved on to heckle other people.

Pluto has a way of dredging up all those dark dirty little secrets into the Light, so they can be consciously viewed and released. Pluto's energies allow for detoxification and transmutation of those things previously hidden. The Moon represents our emotional nature. Put these two planets' energies together in opposition, and you have the most powerful, transforming emotional transit one can endure.

Strangely, for the previous one and one-half years I had thought, "Hey, this Pluto/Moon opposition stuff isn't that tough." Yes, I had noticed a few small power struggles, and other unfinished stuff manifesting in my day-to-day life, but nothing of any size.

Suddenly I realized what was happening. This heavy darkness approaching had broken into my conscious awareness, finally released from the subconscious where it had been conveniently stuffed for God knows how long. It had taken one and one-half years of this strong transit influence to wear down my resistance to facing whatever this was. I felt a cold chill as I turned and looked into this darkness.

I sat quietly where I would be undisturbed, closed my eyes, and began to open my pores to sense what this thing was. It felt like a thick blanket of insulating material lying over the "floor" of an area within myself. Curious about what was underneath, in my mind's eye I began to gently lift the edge. As the barrier responded to the pressure I was exerting, I began to hear a small child sobbing deeply.

Immediately I recognized her as myself! I was coming upon the living essence of my pure, inner child. "What is it Kristi, what's wrong? Why are you crying?" I asked. She could not answer. She just looked at me from her tear-stained face.

As we looked into each other's eyes, I began to hear muffled voices coming from the thick dark blanket now above us. As I strained to hear the words, I felt the feeling first. A heartfelt piercing pain made up of critical words cut into my Being.

All at once, hurtful childhood experiences flooded back clearly into my consciousness. It would be late; I would be watching TV in the living room where I grew up. I would have been asked once before to go to bed. Of course, there were better things to do, and I would have ignored the request. Into my mind would come the strong message: "Time to go to bed, now!"

Before my body could respond, the words would come audibly from one of my parents. I would say, "I was just going to..." and the laughter would start. It had become a family joke: "I know, you were just going to!" Well you see: I *was just going to.* My telepathic ability was working well, and the loudness of the message could not be ignored. But the real explanation was lost in the mockery of a lying child. So over time, the mind messages silenced, and the joke (at my expense) was forgotten.

The strength of the feelings lying in this dark hidden corner within myself stunned me. I marveled at how many phrases and experiences were stuck here in perpetual replay. This sweet pure child was smothered and suspended in this quagmire of insults and reproaches.

I looked back at my parents as they were in my childhood. In an instant I knew my father's voice delivered most of these hurtful comments. I had always felt I could never do anything well enough to suit him, never quite measuring up to his expectations. He was not a man of many words. It had always seemed a grand shame that most of the words he did direct toward me struck my ears in disapproving tones.

I felt shaken. I thought these things were long forgiven and forgotten. I love my father. He has mellowed wonderfully with the years. As an adult, I know his true love and respect for me. I had never suspected that a young tender part of me was stuck in the old way of being, dreadfully in need of a healing.

I put my arms around Kristi, and we hugged as our hearts poured into each other. The hurt and tears welled up as I came back in synch with my forgotten past. I knew the way to heal this old hurt was through forgiveness. I needed to forgive my father for saying these things so painfully received by my young self. I also needed to forgive myself for having allowed this excruciating pain to remain unresolved for so many years. This layer of heavy darkness had to be cleared! I opened my mouth and came the words…"*I forgive myself. I forgive my father, Stanley Ralph Knapp.*"

As I said these words aloud, slowly repeating them, I could feel a sensation in my solar plexus. It felt as if a weed with an incredibly complex root system was being slowly and firmly pulled from my center. A physical change was happening within my body.

After the space of one or two minutes, the sensation subsided, and I felt done. I looked again at the dark blanket and visualized it disintegrating. My imagination sprang forth and began to frolic in different ways to get the job done. I saw silver sparkles that danced on the darkness, dissolving it wherever they landed. I saw a big piece being stuffed into a large wooden trunk, and dropped over the stern of a large fishing boat, *kersplash* and it was gone!

The wide variety of visions and scenarios continued until the dark blanket was no more. I opened my eyes slowly and sat very still at the edge of exhaustion.

A week or so after this experience, I shared this story with my parents over the telephone. Three thousand pesky miles separated us; the phone was as close as we could come for the moment. I love them deeply, and I knew they would share my joy at having had this incredibly freeing experience. I also felt the importance of being open about what I had uncovered.

I grew up in a time when talking candidly—child-with-parent—was not typical. I wanted to knock down any last vestiges of taboo subjects, to allow all things to be open for discussion. And I wanted my father to have an opportunity to know the repercussions of those critical words that came so easily for him.

After sharing the experience over the phone, we cried and laughed, and marveled together at what an amazing occurrence it had been. Through tears, my mother flooded forth with other memories from my childhood and her own, sharing words and situations that had caused pain and distress.

My father laughed, because he had used the very phrase in question only hours earlier. He had coaxed my mother as she worked up the courage to move through her physical therapy exercises, part of her recuperation from knee surgery. Strangely, the joke of "you were just going to..." was truly funny. We laughed together in a new atmosphere of honesty and clarity of meaning.

The valuable gifts presented in that quiet evening of introspection and release have been many. I now know how to search out and destroy icky junk from the hidden corners of myself. One bit more salve had been applied to my relationship with my parents, ensuring truthfulness and closeness as fellow actors and friends. And best of all, I now have a new best friend.

Kristi was always there. I had been receiving her silly ideas that helped me remember to have fun. However, I had not seen her since I was her age. The term "Inner Child" had been nothing but an intellectual idea before. Now she is a living breathing part of me, never to be forgotten or abandoned again. She is there whenever I look for her.

She does not cry anymore. We can play and laugh, hug and love each other. I am finding that she knows my guides better than I do. The child is truly closest to God! Together, we feel very much like a family.

I knew time had come to reunite. At least forty-six years had passed since we were one. I now understand why we can hit a wall in our development. Unless this beautifully pure innocent Being is a real active part of our conscious selves, we have to pause until we remember, and integrate their energy into ours. We must return to our innocence to be most able to flow with the natural currents in our life. How can we see things as fresh and new when we have forgotten how to do this? Our inner child ALWAYS remembers.

Joyful expectancy in life can bubble up into your consciousness, drawing attention to the nebulous feeling that something is going to happen. It gives us an early warning, allowing us to shift some of our awareness into long-range scanners: to keep an eye out. This is all part of being healthy and alive. This is the only place where expectation is appropriate.

Are your expectations neutral when you meet someone new, waiting for the experience to unfold into the most it can be? Or do you look at their dress, their shoes, the hairstyle and begin to categorize their *type*, even before a first word is spoken? If someone you know has ever surprised you, then you have experienced an event with this person that proved wrong a preconceived idea. It is hard for any actor in physical expression to be free of this common shortcoming.

Now pause for a moment and look at yourself. You know who you are. You know what you are good at doing, and what you are not. You know what you like, and what you do not. But how do you know this? And why would you **ever** think you know all there is to know about yourself?

You are an evolving work-in-progress. If you expect yourself to act in certain ways in certain settings, then you are limiting what might be. Leave your preconceived ideas of who you are, and how you act, in your personal history book, that is where it belongs: in the past. There are no rules saying that your choice of a particular action in the past requires the same behavior today.

We are truly meant to be adventurers. There is always the possibility of something familiar happening in a new way. At any time, you can find something you have never noticed before that intrigues you. When you close your heart to such possibilities, you shift into automatic. You miss fresh experiences. You just do not see them. This is why experiencing life with your inner child pops your daily life into multidimensional living. Through a child's eyes, expectations do not exist. Everything is new, fresh, and an adventure. Even fear is a word that holds no meaning.

I find it much easier to play now. Fewer things seem serious. If Kristine forgets how to dance with joy, Kristi reminds me and leads the way. If Kristine gets bogged down in physical world concerns, Kristi grabs my hand and pulls me away. Even mountainous problems transform into "little things," as the resolutions present themselves as our life unfolds. I have learned that together, as one, we can flow naturally through the swirling currents of life.

I am prepared for whatever comes. Knowing that any moment can bring new surprises, has me living with my heart in my throat. Kristi sees beauty and wonder everywhere. Everything is exciting and fresh: a butterfly, cold milk from the refrigerator, a dry set of clothes when an unexpected shower soaks you to the bone. ***Nothing is taken for granted!***

Can you imagine a child never losing touch with their inner innocence and joy as they grow to adulthood? Can you imagine the loving and sensitive parenting required to accomplish such a gentle rearing? Perhaps with wisdom and patience, more of us can learn to lay tender hands upon those new souls entrusted to our care.

If you do not have your inner child on tap, start searching inside. The child is there: an integral part of your healthy whole Self. I know between God's Love and Kristi's joy, there is no worry.

T E N

My Five-Year Plan

I HAVE SPENT MANY YEARS in the corporate work world. Here, the annual task of quantifying one's expected direction and results has always clashed with my personal beliefs. Pressed to create such a document, I found myself laboring to find general words that would allow the specifics of the future time, to finish the thoughts with the created details.

As the concept of *letting go and letting God* has become a real part of my Being, I can now say: **"I have no plan."** I admit there are broad areas of interest that have come to my notice. These are subjects that I am curious about, and would like to spend some time exploring. But there is no plan written down, no rules about where or how my life is moving.

As I have stated before, our sequential sense of time is a physical-existence sensation. If you are fortunate enough to perceive a sense of timelessness while in physical form, you begin to get the idea that everything does exist in the NOW. The trick is to focus on making those choices, in every moment, to express yourself as you truly wish. Once you are doing this, you are *living*.

Since you are always in the NOW, there is no need to be concerned about quantifying tomorrow. Tomorrow is the NOW you will be in then. Between NOW and then is a continuous flow of NOWs. The only trick to living wisely, is to appreciate and accept each NOW, as you focus consciously within it.

So, as I am busy today expressing myself, new yearnings come to my notice. Once I tune in to my heart, and open to messages from my higher-self, those possibilities in harmony with my true Self will come bubbling up into consciousness.

Life is like a candy store: pick what feels right, and move toward it. If it is right for you, each step will flow effortlessly. Instead, if your way becomes filled with obstacles and difficulties, than it is not for you. *Least resistance IS your path!* Do not worry, there is lots more to choose from. **Life IS this simple.**

ELEVEN

Why Isn't Living From A Spiritual Focus More Popular?

WHEN ONE CONSCIOUSLY NOTICES what is happening in one's life, and makes moment-by-moment decisions naturally based on inclinations flowing from one's heart and beyond, one is living from a spiritual focus. Life flows, is accepted and enjoyed.

Walking confidently without seeing the solid ground on which your next footfall will rest, is also part of the process. You live free of fears, confident of success, while not predetermining the next step. Opportunities to advance to your next life situation appear, as they are appropriate. You know that it is in the Divine Plan for the Universe to support your needs, desires, and intentions.

To remain in balance with your natural spiritual Self, you want to feel a sense of willingness to embrace anything appearing in your life. An overtone of acceptance, non-judgment, and Love will be your main frame of mind. Even though free will is granted as our greatest gift, you freely choose not to use it. God's Will and your will are the same. You let go, and let God.

Having said this, it is easy to see that our physical world does not support or encourage such "irresponsible" behavior. The unspoken rules are always pushing at us. If we have not decided what our vocation will be by the time we are in the last years of our public school, we are shirking our duty. We must know where we are going, and how we intend to get there, or we are shiftless and lazy. If we manipulate or use another person to enhance our way, we are merely being clever. Success is measured in net worth. Charitable works are what you do for tax breaks. Spouses must be sexy, and always at our disposal. We alter our behavior to elevate how others will think of us.

Truly, living from a Spiritual focus does not match this mold. However, just because a relaxed natural life style is not the typical stereotype of a successful 20th century human, it does not make it wrong. It simply makes it unusual.

In today's off-center Western world, it is difficult to truly connect with one's own essence. With so many people piled together, each in the midst of their own Play, there are many energies jumbled together. While finding personal ways to close out this static, the door to our inner world can be illusive.

One way to begin trusting your ability to have conscious self-awareness, is to *know* your own expression is safe from melding into the crowd. Your energy always remains intact, even when you open to subtle realities.

The following are two separate functions naturally accomplished by our energy systems: (1) the filtering out of disruptive energy to maintain our personal balance in the mayhem, and (2) opening our awareness to the subtle realms. Both are appropriate to the individual, although they can seem an odd couple.

Our body's system naturally accommodates our needs, and functions on many levels to support our desires.

If you feel overwhelmed by the chaos in today's world, you are not alone. Most of the frenzied activity, swirling in the quest for success and fulfillment, is *not* marching to a natural rhythm. It is created from a combination of ego bent on power, advertising ploys bent on dollars, and distorted truths presented to manipulate the masses.

The only view that provides hope, comes from realizing that the population is made up of individuals. Over our own individual self we have complete dominion. Each individual has the personal power to turn aside from the pattern accepted by society. Instead of following what is typically encouraged, we can choose to move naturally in synch with the Universe.

By being true to ourselves in every moment, we break away from the swift crazy current, to find a quiet eddy in which to consider ourselves and the purpose of our Play. By personally dropping out of the stampede, we strengthen the higher vibration of personal awareness on our planet. We also weaken the energy of mindless group-following one bit more.

I feel confident that the day will come when Humanity will remember its united consciousness. When this day arrives, our societal facade will drop away. We will each look into one another's eyes with a new appreciation, recognition and fondness. Once the concocted rules crumble, we will find clear guidance from our natural instincts. Our knowledge that we all are One, will reclaim center Stage.

But for now, when everyone is "spitting on the sidewalk," and society approves, it can be a lonely feeling when such behavior does not match your natural inclination. The interesting fact is that many people would prefer not to "spit on the sidewalk." Their peers and employers expect it, so the personal nature is suppressed, and the pressure to act as expected is given its head.

Many people are in the spiritual closet. Often we lack opportunity to visibly move in gentler ways while finding support from society. Becoming an object of ridicule is a scary prospect.

HOLD ON. What is this? Is every person really poised waiting for me to make a mistake, so they might point and make fun? What about their own Plays? Aren't there lots more important things in their lives that draw their attention? Would my world really come tumbling down around my ears if I said aloud "Thank you, God" when something went better than expected at work? Get real folks!

It is my experience that although you may get a strange look from some people, everyone receives a "Thank you, God" comment very personally. Those within earshot are granted one grain more courage to let their own closeted feelings come closer to the surface in their daily expression.

One of the finest things you can do is be constantly true to you. Your example can have deeper impact than you imagine. It lays the groundwork for others to adopt a more open spiritual approach in their lives. Make it a point to be open about your position.

To provide an example of someone who moves in harmony with the Divine plan, allow your words and deeds to flow freely. The energy that you emit will touch others on a non-verbal level. They will be drawn to freer behavior as a moth is drawn to a flame. Pure, free flowing energy is a fountain of youth for the Soul.

When we are honest with one another, a great deal of energy is made available. During a conversation with someone, if a concern comes into your mind, deal with it promptly. It is most efficient (energy-wise) to ask the question, receive the answer, resolve, and release the concern before continuing. You free yourself of the distraction, and allow your focus to remain cleanly in the NOW.

When you handle things as they come up, moment-to-moment, all your energy is available and focused on what is happening. A group of people exchanging ideas as they develop a joint decision, handling each issue before they continue, forms an extremely exhilarating atmosphere. You can feel the creative flow of energy in the room, witnessing their honest connection with each other.

No social setting is important enough to supersede the benefits of addressing each question as it is revealed. It is like settling for constipation, when we know regular bowels allow our whole Being to feel much better. The drain on our energy system is very much akin to a toxin in our physical body. They are both unnatural conditions that take a toll when they are retained over time, instead of being released.

Can you even imagine a world in which no reasons exist to hold secrets, or to tell lies to protect something from discovery? Maybe we could dedicate a special day where everyone solemnly vowed to tell only the truth, as they knew it. We could call it *"Honesty Day."* Everyone not capable of honoring this Day's spirit, would be required to stay at home. We would know we could say anything our heart requested, of anyone we encountered.

To celebrate the mission of Honesty Day, everyone not at home would also agree to receive all questions lovingly. We would answer each question with as much honesty as possible in a clear response.

Can you just imagine the rush of unfettered energy swirling around so many clean exchanges between people? I can only believe it would be a Day talked about for some time.

With practice, we can perfect ways in which we are true to our need for expression, while softening our language out of love and caring for the other person. It is a communication goal well worth pursuing. The less energy wasted, the more energy is available to propel us forward into our blossoming story line, while illuminating possibilities for others by our example.

We are each unique. The experiences sketched into our scripts to facilitate our individual growth are as unique as we are. Allow everyone their own perspectives and beliefs. You wish the same for yourself.

If someone else is not interested in what you have to say, let it be. Do not alter your own behavior or direction to spend energy attempting to talk someone into something in which they are not interested. Live your life as you know to be true to your basic nature. The most appropriate reply you can offer others, who are seeking their own answers, is to just be yourself in everything that you do, and say.

Why Is There Good And Bad?

THE TRUE ANSWER TO THIS QUESTION is simply: we have made a choice to label some things "good," some things "bad." Truthfully, everything simply IS. The framework of our everyday life is simply a web of Love vibration that supports any and all creations we actors manifest.

Our Stage is brought to us through the loving generosity of Divine Oneness. When we decide to recognize things as separate elements, and then further define them with labels of "good" or "bad," these labels are also our creations. Placing a label of "good" or "bad" on anything is a judgment from our ego-mind. Yet even this act of judging something is neither *good* nor *bad*.

The mind becomes very quiet when one stops feeling the need to pass judgment on people and events. Such a mindset makes this additional time available for more positive pursuits.

As you release your need to judge, you take on a natural stance of unconditional love and acceptance. Not only do you lose your desire to label, but you gently support the right of things to be as they are. Since you only associate directly with those things in harmony with yourself, things of different vibration have nothing to do with you. It is very appropriate you just let them be. By labeling them "bad," and giving them time in your mind, you are not writing them out of your script.

So know that one actor's "good" is another actor's "bad," and one actor's "bad" is considered "good" by another. Each human soul upon the planet has come with his own script and perspective. Each is at a different point in their soul's journey. Some are very young and dwell in the more coarse vibrations of the darker-side of life. Each of us lives by our God-given right to create and follow our own story line, wherever it may lead.

As incarnations are lived, you become more accustomed to the energies found in the physical. What attracted you before, due to its dangerous and exciting nature, begins to repel you as you sense it has no lasting benefit for the individuals involved. You become more interested in, and attracted to, energy of a higher frequency.

No matter how evolved, at some point each actor has taken the life of another without remorse. Perhaps you fired your rifle into a group of Indians on horseback, as they galloped around your circled wagons. We have come here in Play to experience it all, and we have done all. No actor is better than another. Each is loved equally.

A major reason for this difference in behavior is found in the soul's age. The younger soul, having lived fewer lifetimes, is more involved in coarse energies that affect and interfere with others. An older soul is not as interested in banging up against other actors. They are more curious about their own development and purpose, often leading very quiet simple lives.

We will all—in one life or another—be everyone imaginable, at every point along the spectrum. To support our various roles in our many lifetimes, our personal characteristics will have run a full gamut: male, female, every skin color imaginable, heterosexual, homosexual, bisexual, celibate, sighted, blind, deaf, etc.

If our actions greatly impact and influence other actors, we create bits of karma. We will carry these IOUs for as many lifetimes as it takes before we each decide with one another "to pay the debt," and bring the ledger into balance. This is the only true celestial justice.

Although we may have no accurate conscious memory of karma, we will participate in events that will resolve these imbalances. We will find ourselves involved with actors and situations where we may do a favor for no known reason, even for someone we barely know (in this lifetime). We may find good fortune when least expected, as our scale tipped in the opposite direction is balanced.

Karma is nothing more than some charged energy particles that we carry in our essence, until a balance is struck in an exchange of give and take. Even in resolving karma, there is no "good" or "bad" involved. The event simply allows energies to find a resolution, equalization and balance.

Although "good" and "bad" are most accurately described as worldly subjective matters, the existence of Light and Dark is quite a different issue. Light, the higher vibration of Divine Existence, is one end of the vibrational spectrum. At the other end is Darkness, exemplified by a low vibration of coarser energy. Neither Light nor Darkness can exist where the other does. Every one and every thing exists somewhere on the scale between these two poles.

As an actor makes choices in harmony with his life's purpose, while moving towards a more evolved state, the more *Light* comes into his Being. Some actors choose to live with both feet firmly planted in the physical world, without concern for personal evolution. They find many tempting diversions that can easily lure them into falling further from grace, and embracing the *Dark*.

Yet even with this evidence of two directions one can choose to move, there is no "good" or "bad" involved. It is true that as one's Being increases in vibration, becoming more enLIGHT-ened, the actor is moving closer to God. If one follows the other path, they are retreating from being in God's presence. God is Light. God's pure unconditional Love for us cannot be distinguished from the purest white Light.

Yet if no Darkness existed, there would be nothing from which to differentiate the Light. All we encounter in the physical is perceived within a dichotomy: male and female, ying and yang, love and hate, North and South, hot and cold, bitter and sweet, etc. No matter how enlightened we become, we each have a shadow side as long as we are in physical form.

We each harbor dark fears, hidden away in our subconscious. The memories in our cells contain unforgiven hurt from the past. As we face and make our choices in this life, our heart and conscience—our voice from beyond—easily tells us the level of Light or Dark involved. Experiences brimming with joy, carry us toward the Light. Experiences filled with elements such as hatred or cruelty, pull our vibration lower.

If you find yourself in dark situations that seem to have power over you, remember the Darkness cannot remain if you bring in the Light. Tell the truth about a situation. Bring all hidden agendas into the open to allow the Sun to shine in. You can disarm even a strong fear, if you look upon it unfalteringly in the Light of truth. Many fears depend on your unwillingness to examine them in order to maintain their control. They hide in your dark corners.

Things of the Dark linger and become heavy, dirty, rancid, moldy, etc. They stay far past their usefulness and slow our progress.

Things of the Light are in themselves light in weight. They appear when appropriate, serve their purpose, and are released. They leave us one bit wiser, more joyful, or more capable of finding our next natural step. We are unhindered, leaving yesterday's baggage at yesterday's train station.

To move toward enlightenment, we must each look in our dark corners for memories from the past (and present) that need releasing. Forgiveness is the strongest tool for unclasping their hold, and telling them to be gone. Forgiveness is not only for others, but also for ourselves. Offering forgiveness frees us from the ties that have bound us with people and experiences. It offers freedom for bondage.

> *I forgive myself. I forgive everyone, everything, every memory, every experience in need of forgiveness, from the past and present. I forgive all these things NOW!*

Words of this sort throw open the shutters, allowing the light to stream in. Such statements release dark particles from our bodies, even when we have no conscious knowledge of the details of each thing dissolved. The power in the spoken word can unlock doors to freedom.

THIRTEEN

Why Ask Why?

QUESTIONS ARE TRICKY LITTLE THINGS. Look to your internal state when a question comes forward in your mind. Are you feeling deadly serious at your core? Do you feel on the edge of exploding because your emotions have you in an intense turmoil? Are you more interested in what someone will think of you for asking the question, than you are in the answer?

If the answer is "Yes" to any of these, then you are off on a tangent with old Mr. Ego in the saddle. In such cases your mind's activity has probably taken center stage. Any forthcoming answer would be lost in its shadow.

Instead, you may be gently pondering recent events in your mind. Your question, as a quiet inquiry, is carefully seeking the sense-memory of each event, while your mind searches for a pattern to yield a new understanding. Here, you are simply in the process of living.

Asking questions is a way of resolving and releasing a sense of concern or focus that has brought the natural flow of our life to a pause. It is best to deal with a question when it is first noticed.

Imagine you are having a conversation with someone, and a question comes to mind. Instead of handling the question directly, you may choose a less efficient method. You might decide to observe the conversation for hints that would answer your question. You might disregard the concern and suppress it. Any way you handle it *other* than directly, will drain energy from your primary effort of having an honest exchange of ideas.

When you duck dealing with questions as they come up, you end up dragging tendrils of unfinished business around. You will look at this unfinished stuff later, trying to decide if it is important enough to get it answered, or to toss it away.

However, once the scene in which this question came up has passed, the whole energy setting will be different. And this old issue will have been puttering around your mind for a while. It will have been given some of your energy, and will have developed a bit of life of its own. Finding its resolution, and releasing it, becomes more difficult.

Sometimes, knowing of whom to ask your question can be a major challenge. Never overlook yourself as a source for your answers. Everyone relates to life from their own perspective. The same question will receive different answers depending on who is asked. When you ask it of yourself, you will get the most appropriate answer, because no translation between personal perspectives will be required. The way you use language will be consistent between your question and your answer. There is also a wonderful depth of other Beings, guides and higher-self who have a breadth of knowledge you would not easily find in other actors. When you ask yourself, you open to a broader source of answers.

I once knew someone who shared an experience that illustrates this. She told me how she was in an automobile with a friend on the freeway. As they chatted, she mentioned that she had a sizable amount of money she wanted to invest, but she was having trouble deciding which stock to purchase. She said something like, "I wish I had a good tip so my investment would grow strongly…" At that moment, she looked out the side window of the car at the truck passing. "FRITO LAY" was on the side of the truck in large red letters. *She even made the conscious connection between her question and the words she read!*

But it was a passing notice, and she let the door of opportunity close without stepping through its portal. You see, she had this experience in the early years of this company's existence. As with so many at startup, their stock was available at a very reasonable price. Needless to say, it was good advice.

The most useful questions come up naturally, stimulated by the events unfolding in one's life. Many will have answers that flow in just as naturally on the heels of the question. We are simply consciously watching the dynamics of our spiritual self in expression.

As a small child questions, a wise person guiding his development offers a simple response with loving clarity. An answer is always given, even if the answer is: "It is outside your ability to experience an answer at this time" or "It is outside your energy scope" or "There is no answer to your question."

Often, this is the quality of the answer you receive when you ask a question of the Universe. The silence you mistakenly take for no response is asking you to have patience with Divine timing. If your question has validity within the scope of your script, you will receive an answer, when the time is right. The answer may come as a life event that yields a new understanding. Trust that all knowledge needed in your Being will be provided when the time is appropriate.

Since we have wonderfully creative minds, we can become emotionally involved with our process of questioning. In our more formalized seeking professions, such as pure mathematics or research sciences, actors may begin following a series of questions and answers. They may feel hot on the scent of discovery, when a roadblock appears. They face a brick wall with no apparent way around, over, or through. It takes a very aware actor to release the hunt, relax, and sit back.

Being brought to a standstill without an answer, *is an answer* in its own right. We are constantly guided. Everything that occurs is in response to our life's creative flow.

If you are brought up short with nowhere to go, step back and shift gears. If reviewing your most recent string of questions and answers brings you to the same obstacle, choose a brand new approach. Even dropping the subject of the question, and throwing your attention into another area, may be what is needed.

If the ultimate answer that you so actively pursued embraces the highest good for all concerned, you will find it. It may pop out at you when least expected, perhaps as you flow down another seemingly unrelated mental path.

Recognize the appearance of resistance in your life as feedback when a change of approach is appropriate. Find an area

where your energy flows unrestrictedly, and you have found
your next natural course of action.

An astronomical event occurred Thursday, September 26,
1996, which gave me the feeling that it would be a special day
for me. The reason may have been that so many celestial events
would occur on this one particular afternoon and evening.

First, the planet Mercury went Direct in the early afternoon
after a very trying three weeks of Retrograde. Next, the moon
lost its Void of Course as it moved into Aries. Aries is the first
astrological sign, and the first House of the astrological chart.
It represents the *I AM* God presence energy, the most personal
area of the chart. A little after 9:00 p.m., the final full Lunar
Eclipse of this century started. The eclipse culminated around
10:00 p.m. when the last light of the sun left its surface. One
hour later, the Harvest Moon became Full in its lunar cycle.

I had arranged to go to a metaphysical bookstore with a
friend, for a Full Moon ceremony. By 9:00 p.m., I knew the
evening would be far too potent to allow distraction by social
requirements of a group. I excused myself and left.

During the drive home my excitement began to increase.
I called Lee briefly to make sure he had remembered the eclipse.
Lee was where he could watch, and was enjoying it as well. I had
seen lunar eclipses before, but for some reason this one seemed
special.

When I arrived home, I left all of the lights out, found the
binoculars, and went out to the backyard to view the moon. By
around 9:20 p.m. I could see the darkened bite into the lower
left edge of the moon's form.

As the process of the eclipse slowly commenced, I was gently guided to immerse myself in the water of our swimming pool, which reflected the moon's luminous light from above. As I felt the warm waters around my body and watched the light slowly dim on the ripples, I felt immersed in the feminine aspect of the moon reflecting down upon the Earth. The vibrant male in the heavens—our Sun—was streaming forth in all its continuous glory, ever further below the Earth's horizon behind which it had disappeared, more than two hours before.

Here we were on this beautiful green and blue globe, suspended between our astronomical male and female elements. We were enjoying a lunar eclipse from our hemisphere, while the moon viewed a solar eclipse from her perspective in space.

The physical atmosphere around me felt alive with Nature. The wind gently pushed through the woods behind our house, producing a rustling whoosh song that lent the dimension of sound to my experience. I felt the near presence of animals, birds, and those Nature spirits attending the beautiful area where our home was located.

As the bright reflection of the sun's light receded from the moon's surface, her true beauty struck me. Through our atmosphere, her color appeared golden tinged with red. She did not appear cold and lifeless. The fullness of her globe and gentle Being touched me deeply.

I had not often enjoyed her for herself. She usually moved quietly, dutifully reflecting back the sun's light, which was mistakenly taken for an expression of herself.

Tonight she glowed down upon my vision with her own quality fully apparent. I felt appreciative of her company in a way I had not found reason to know before. Her quality was of gentle constancy. She moved slowly, willingly doing that which had been destined for her to do, without fanfare or fuss.

The next morning, Lee made notice of how fitfully I had slept. Thinking myself to have slept soundly, I wondered what had been taking place, as he told me of the odd noises I was making in my sleep.

The day seemed new (or was it me?) I found it easy to know myself as a spiritual Being, as the events of the day brought peels of giggles and silliness. I felt a subtle new depth in my Being. I looked forward to more understanding coming from the special touch I had received the previous night.

I had not questioned "What will this day bring to me?" nor do I suspect I could have put its answer into words. All I knew, was what would happen this day would be special for me. Trusting in this knowledge, all that was necessary was to be aware, and receptive.

Sometimes questions can disrupt our knowing in the natural flow and quality of events. Questions must come softly, welling up as a supportive element in the conscious awareness of the moment. If they are brazen and loud, they can destroy our grasp on that which they have come to question. Pushy questions serve to muddy the waters, rather than allow our Being to absorb the deeper meanings of the moment in silent observation.

Often questions will come up because an old pattern is failing. A question forms because the technique or subject matter at focus was originally constructed by an ego's perception, and is crumbling due to its own unnatural structure. The *question* is simply our uneasiness with something we sense to be unnatural. Life is extremely simple. When lived as it comes with willing acceptance, very few questions come up in one's mind.

Questions like "Is O.J. Simpson really innocent?" are not worth your notice. Every event serves a purpose, or the actors involved would not have created it. Every person has a unique perception of the event. There are as many versions of opinions, as there are actors giving it attention in their lives. A real answer to such a question is just not important. No one answer will satisfy everyone.

Many actors who spend their time peering into other actor's lives, judging and questioning, pointing and offering their opinions, are hiding from the more appropriate action of living their own life. Whatever floats your boat. It is your script, you can do with it what you want. There is no right or wrong way to live your life. There is only the way you choose to live it.

It has always seemed a bit silly to me when two people get together and have an argument over their difference of opinion. You see, if each of them truly believes their own opinion is correct, then *they are right*. From each of their perspectives, as best their trusty minds can detect, each has correctly evaluated the question.

Despite what other people think, it is only your own perspective that deserves your attention. Questions asked of yourself are valuable because they help you hone your perspective. It does not matter what someone else thinks.

It is a great honor to be asked a question by another actor. They are asking you about a subject on which they feel your insight might give them some missing clarity. Take the time to listen carefully to what they are asking. Many of our interactions with one another are scenes we have woven into the tapestry of our lives to bring growth to both participants.

Perhaps the question being asked is one you have forgotten to ask of yourself. Allow the exchange of energy between the two of you to find an answer that serves the highest good in each of you. Of course, there are always those questions that are little other than recreation: "What do you think, is O.J. really innocent?" Nothing earth-shattering here.

I was at a professional gathering one evening. The individual sitting beside me had some announcements he wanted to make to the group. He was obviously quite nervous about speaking before the assembled people. He was asking me questions about what he should say, and how he should say it. He was saying aloud what many a nervous actor might have been mumbling to himself, silently in the mind. He was spending so much energy being concerned about what he should do, that he was unable to just BE.

When his turn to say a few words arrived, he faltered and mumbled. The information he provided was mostly lost in the nervous condition he was most successfully portraying and experiencing. Bless his soul. He did not understand it did not matter what anyone thought. When sharing information, the simple act of opening one's mouth and trusting what is needed will be provided works! I wondered what he might have done with all the energy expended, if he had been free of his self-reproach and self-doubt.

But there is no such thing as a mistake or accident. I further wondered why the Universe had brought this actor to this place that evening, to so clearly portray this "nervousness-in-front-of-a-group." I wondered which actors attending had received a dose of understanding that furthered their own growth.

Yes, there are questions to be asked…"Why was *this* brought to my notice?""Why doesn't my anger or fear just go away when I ignore it?""Why am I sick? What insight am I to gain?" The way you evaluate the question, before turning your attention elsewhere in search of its answer, can bring you a great deal of personal self-knowledge.

With practice, you may feel like you are playing a personal version of the television game show "Jeopardy." Your answers come in the form of your questions. You naturally have at your disposal great wisdom and knowledge. Pay close attention to your questions, listen carefully, and be ready to receive your answers.

What Are My Responsibilities?

WHAT DO YOU WANT TO DO? If you are attached to friends who have strong ideas of what to do and where to go, do their ideas make sense for you? Do their ideas make your heart honestly sing with as much joy or purpose as your friends seem to feel?

Have you ever sat quietly, and asked yourself what it is **you** want to do? What thought of an activity within your mind enlivens your heart and excites you? Are you already incorporating this activity into your life, or have you not yet found time for it?

You have come here to express those traits and live the experiences you sketched into your script, before your Play began. If once here you duck this responsibility and go to sleep, moving through each day in a fixed pattern, it is only you who will mind. It is your script. You are your only real critic. When the curtain is down, you will provide your own review. And even this will be done in a loving, objective fashion.

Since all things are connected, every choice you make—every word, thought and deed—impacts on the Whole. Not only is your future path affected as you dynamically alter your script, but every other actor makes his adjustments. It is the hidden symphony of interrelations of energy.

When you carry forth lovingly, you move with full realization of your influence. You are not only responsible for everything you perceive as happening directly to yourself, but you also take greater care and thought in those actions you express that impact on others. These "others" include all living things, including our beautiful Mother Earth herself.

The choices you make take on a grand scope. If you buy the clever new product manufactured at the cost of blowing many tons of pollutants into our atmosphere, you are supporting energy contrary to what you know to be supportive of our ecology.

If you own the manufacturing firm producing this new product, and your reason is a more substantial profit, your direct non-supportive impact on our world is even more obvious. The farther from Nature's balance your choices take you, the greater degree of karmic energy is created to repay later. This is just a natural by-product of such decisions.

But your choices are your own. What other actors think, say or do does not matter. It is what *you* think and feel that produce your choices. Your responsibility in these matters is your inalienable right. Your primary responsibility is to *be true to yourself*. To be in touch with your own heart, and direct your script gently. The closer to this mark you manage, the more flowing and easy your life becomes.

So much of what happens in our physical world springs into being as if through mob mentality. No one remembers who originally thought of the idea, or where it started. No one stands up and claims credit or responsibility for it. All anyone knows is: there is a predetermined way of doing something. The acceptance of the masses enforces its reality. The history of repetition somehow assigns the action validity. Rigid patterns form, and the individual's spontaneous creative spark is retarded.

In such a setting, it seems difficult to get to know and express one's true Self. Most people express themselves in thought, word and deed, based on what others expect of them. The focus is external. To create the desired appearance, considerable effort is expended in acquiring possessions. Somehow, accumulating material things of a particular sort is supposed to define one's value and essence.

However material things come and go as sure as the sun rises and sets. It is the individual's natural expression that is constant. This spiritual essence at our core forms a stable base from which to experience life.

The less attention given to the noisy, flashy distractions that dazzle your conscious senses while in physical form, the more you will begin to pick up on your subtle personal rhythm, and move forward with confidence. Once you are on the scent, it becomes progressively easier to know what choices feel right to you.

Do not let me make this sound dull: there will be plenty of fun along the way. We have taken on this physical body to experience the physical world through our senses. The feelings we have in our bodies are important to fully experience and acknowledge.

When an actor appears to change, it is because he is slowly discarding extraneous bits, while moving more into accord with his central purpose. Meditation can help serve to get one in touch with what the real you feels like.

When your eyes are closed and you are in a peaceful environment, your true essence flows forward to greet you. As you become familiar with its rhythm, leading your life more in tune with your personal style becomes easier. You find making choices becomes more natural, and you waste less time second-guessing yourself on past decisions.

As you become synchronized with your true Self, you need not doubt ideas that come up in your mind. If the thought is not handed to you from the outside physical world, you create it. If it arrives clothed in gentle calmness, be assured your heart and beyond have brought you this gift. If you move forward, making decisions flavored by the ideas coming into you through these natural channels, you will continue to bring your expression into accord (a-chord) with the real you.

However if you feel stalled and not sure what your next step is, ask for help. God is always ready to lend a hand. Asking for assistance comes from a genuine desire to realign your direction with that naturally intended in your Play.

I find dealing with this subject requires a sensitive and most delicate touch. I must balance my realization of personal soul responsibility for my own choices, against humility in subordinating my will to that of God. I have been granted free will. If I function in harmony with God's Supreme Play, I will freely choose not to use my own will. Instead I will choose to surrender to God's Will. Here is where I find this gets a bit tricky.

If I remain open to guidance, accept and follow my intuition and natural urges, I may seem to be turning into a wishy-washy yes-man. However, we are each a unique expression of God. We are all an inseparable part of the Whole. We are all One with God. God is within us. We are God. So how can it be that I am surrendering my will to myself?

The answer is simple. My separateness from God is an illusion. To make choices that are in accord with my Play's purpose is to simply surrender to the natural flow of intuition that comes into me from the Source. What I do when I relinquish my ego-mind's will is come back into conscious awareness of God's Will, *for this is my own true Will.*

Once doing this, I become anything but wishy-washy. For in moving with these natural urges, I bring the highest expression of my unique God-Self into manifestation. I truly feel passion for living. What I am meant to become in this life comes through with crystal clarity.

We are God. We are each a unique aspect of God in physical expression. When we let go and let God, we flow in natural accord with this God-spark essence in our core. All that is already known within the Whole of God becomes available as needed to easily show us the best choices to embrace. Our script flows gently, bringing those life experiences that facilitate our growth.

It is as important to understand your responsibility for creating your life, as it is to understand where your responsibilities end. An interaction between two actors is a balancing of two individuals in dynamic discovery of themselves. You must respect the boundaries that comprise the other person's Play. Interference or intervention that tries to push or change another actor's script, is not energy well spent. Your karma score card will be busy indeed!

Give the respect due to those you meet, whether you personally understand the path they are on or not. When you look into the eyes of another actor, you are looking into the eyes of another portion of yourself. Each is a unique aspect of God in physical expression. Everything is connected. We are all One.

In today's rushed world, one of the kindest gifts you can give someone is to have patience with them. When your car is in the shop unexpectedly, and you would prefer to be somewhere else, slow down. You are always where you are meant to be. Listen to their explanation of the repair, and smile at them. They are probably tense, waiting for your displeasure to hit their ears in sharp tones. Surprise them with quiet words and reasonable questions. Settle down peacefully in the waiting area. Forgive your vehicle for its failure, the slowness of the mechanic, the awkwardness of the situation. Forgive yourself for having lost patience at first, before you gathered yourself in and remembered to remember yourself as a spiritual Being. Give as you would wish to receive.

When you hear another actor complain and tell story upon story of how their life is sad and difficult, smile gently. They are sharing their perspective of the opportunities active in their life, where their own growth is ready to make some progress. Once they accept what is happening, and look into it for the understanding it is offering, the roadblock will dissolve, and they will move on.

Words of positive encouragement are the best you can offer in such a situation. Perhaps a personal story of how you transmuted a seemingly difficult experience into something learned, resolved and released. However if the meaning of your words is lost on them, you have done all you can to help. Walk away.

We are very privileged to be on our planet at this time. As Lee Carroll channels in the Kryon books, *we all stood in line to be here!* There are only so many bodies to go around, and many souls wishing to be in the physical to experience our planet's transformation first hand.

Each time you offer a kindness instead of an insult, or when you take the time to give someone your undivided attention, you are allowing God's Love energy to flow into our world through your actions. The frequency of our planet's vibration is increased one bit more. The day of Heaven on Earth hastened one moment sooner.

When Do We Know
The Play Was A Success?

MOVE THROUGH EACH MOMENT in accord with your true Self. Then, whenever your curtain comes down, it will finish a balanced well-played performance.

In truth, your Play cannot help but be a success. You had laid out before yourself a grand adventure. As the script evolved, your choices were always your own. Your own creative hand crafted the complexity, or simplicity, chosen in the midst of the dynamics at work. It can be nothing other than a breathtaking composition of your own handiwork.

However society rates your success level as a citizen, your Production can be nothing other than a success. You came. You lived. You grew to one extent or another. All trappings of the physical experience that can seem so important while here, mean NOTHING once your Play has closed. The comparisons used to rate your position in the heap of humanity are but an illusion based on whimsy. All actors are equal. All actors are important. *All actors direct and star in Plays that are successful.*

While we live our lives, what goes on here in the physical takes most of our attention. It takes all we have to remember that we are spiritual Beings, simply Playing on this Stage set for our use. Events mostly seem thrust upon us. It is difficult to preserve one's sense of responsibility for creating all that occurs. When difficult times test our resolve, it takes a great deal of heart and courage to face what is unfolding, and to delve into its meaning so it can be accepted and incorporated. Life goes on.

When I heard about the equestrian accident that paralyzed Christopher Reeve from the neck down, I was shaken. I had always enjoyed his film roles. The quality that came through his portrayals in each movie's story line left me feeling inspired. In a single moment, his whole way of being was changed.

Today I believe, all that went before that moment was for no other purpose than to make many of us aware of the existence of this individual named Christopher Reeves. It is at this point that his service to humanity began.

When an accident or fateful occurrence drastically shifts our ability to function as we have before, it is a tremendous shock to our physical Being. Understand, our soul is well aware of these choices it made coming into this story line. But in our earthly perception, it comes out of nowhere.

A very real sense of mourning is endured for the loss of what was, and for what was naturally expected to continue. The challenge for the actor is in working through to acceptance of the occurrence, and then moving on with the same passion for life as before. For many this challenge can be too much to bear.

Christopher Reeves chose to meet his challenge, to use his new awareness to open other people's eyes. I suspect he has just begun to find the infinite possibilities still open to him, even with the extreme physical limitation his paralysis imposes. What a glorious example he has brought to our world. I honor him for his service.

We are all in the physical here. There can be no Divine Perfection while in this form. We all spend time feeling sorry for ourselves once in a while. The best any of us can ever hope to do is live, consciously aware in every moment. In doing so, we notice all things as they occur. We interact with all actors as the unique spark of God that they are, respecting and honoring them for their purpose for being. We move willingly through our lives, offering love and encouragement to those we meet. We know the importance of always remembering to forgive, especially ourselves.

Through all of Creation there is a perfect balance that is always in place. Everything is always in Divine Right Order. As an actor makes a change in his life, the energy balance of his inner world shifts. A movement in all things in the physical is caused as a new positioning of likes with likes is arranged.

Even during the shift to find a new equilibrium, all things are in perfect balance. During the shift, the energy acting to bring the new equilibrium into synch, strikes the difference needed to retain the perfect balance. This is a bit like which came first, the chicken or the egg? As one's external world shifts to come to agreement with the shift in one's inner world, the quality of the energy interacting during the change maintains the perfect balance. The sum of its parts always equals the same—perfect balance—in every moment.

As Above, so Below. As our inner world's window into those things beyond the physical (Above) refines and evolves through our life experiences, the physical energies that we find expressed in our surroundings (Below) reflect the quality of the inner state. It is not the physical world around us that leads the way, it is our spiritual condition that leads us from within to where we find ourselves each day.

On the day that everyone personally chooses to live without strife, war will cease to exist. The energy of war will no longer have the attention needed to sustain it. As everyone's life conditions shift to support their new loving perspective, the concept of war will no longer have a place on our planet. Achieving peace is not a fight against war. It is achieved simply by embracing peace. And it is so!

As our theatrical experience in the physical draws to an end and the curtain is down, we find that the critics are very gentle and kind. In fact, the hardest (and only) critic to face in a final evaluation of the completed Play, is oneself. Even then, our hero has taken his final curtain call, removed his makeup, and can review his choices and experiences with a fond detachment. Even within the scope of objective evaluation and review there is Love and compassion.

There may have been a nuance of purpose that was lost in the shuffle. In retrospect, if it is important enough, it can be rolled over into the bright beginning of a next script for the next incarnation. For the Play must go on. It's in our blood, you know.

However, there does come a time when our hero pauses and looks back over his varied career. His roles have been extensive, and his experience and wisdom earned expansive. He feels a sense of completion and maturity. The urge to jump into the next production schedule is not a burning desire. Instead, he warms with the feeling of Love for the process, and for those behind-the-scenes Beings who supported and helped his growth while on the Stage.

He begins to understand that his desires are becoming more closely akin to those countless stagehands who assist just outside the spotlight. He knows it is time to be of greater service. His need to refine his individual aspects dissolve into a desire to share his wisdom with other actors in need of counseling and guidance.

Afterword

So you might call what we have here a Spiritual Primer. It is presented to help stimulate you into new levels of investigation and awareness.

The perspectives by which you view this lifetime will be unique among your incarnations. Natural abilities and predisposition may persist, but this point in your Soul's journey is uniquely precious. You are an integral part of the Universe's symphony. As you open to your Play's possibilities and move forward with gay abandon, melodies flow sweeter still.

Many elements in this book were inspired by happenings in my own life, giving my pen impetus to share them with you. I have often felt like a great blue whale slowly swimming through the richness of daily events. With my mouth spread to consciously receive what occurred, digestible bits of information were captured in my filtration system, much as plankton is gathered to sustain the blue giant. From here, these morsels moved as much to feed my soul's growth as to fill the paragraphs and pages of this book.

The process that birthed this book was not merely one individual's effort. Although my perspective has distilled the contents, and has formed many seed ideas seeking your fertile mind, the information herein is from the farthest reaching edges of the Universe. All time, all events, all of life is but hinted at in what is written here.

There is no way to express in words the simple truth of letting loose one's own natural process into manifestation. It is a bit like a roller coaster ride while being blindfolded. The exhilaration and constant surprise refresh and bless one's spirit into eternal radiance and Joy. Riding the wonderful current of NOW allows all concerns to dissolve. The sureness one feels about one's path cancels all extraneous needs for the mind to steal our time. All one has to do is get out of the way!

Your transition can be as slow or as fast as you want. As always, your choices will dictate the speed. You will likely find events and situations bringing to your awareness ideas herein that caught your notice. It is your time to consider some new perspectives, or you would not have read this book and be seeing these words.

These pages warmly challenge you to become alive, to accept and move with the awesome splendor, breadth, and *simplicity* of life. Open to these possibilities and all the world will flow into you. You will no longer be separate, yet you will always have your own unique voice and presence to add.

I am honored and blessed to have come here to share my experiences and perceptions with you. Every word is offered in fellowship and Love.

As we join with our inner child, and boldly ride our trusty tricycle named "Acceptance" through our fears and lessons, we move ever further into the Light, into the infinitely abundant Blessings of God's Love. So come on fellow seekers of the Light...mount up and *LIVE!*

Healing Mantra

*I forgive myself the imperfection
of my humanness, and
I accept my **total Being** as I am NOW.*

*I am a perfect aspect of God
in physical expression.*

I am perfect.

I am.

SPIRITUAL AWARENESS PRODUCTIONS

P.O. Box 519 • Tarpon Springs, FL 34688-0519 • Fax: 727-943-8184
www.SpiritAware.com

Credit Card Orders

Call toll free 1-800-353-3730 Monday-Friday, 8 AM to 5 PM Eastern

☐ VISA ☐ MasterCard ☐ American Express

CARD #: _____ EXPIRES: _____

NAME ON CARD: _____

SIGNATURE: _____

Ordering by Check (payable to *Spiritual Awareness Productions*)

Please send _____ copies of *Dance With The Stars* at $16.95 (U.S.) each.
Add $4.50 Priority Mail shipping for the first book, and 50¢ for each
additional book. Florida residents add sales tax.

Quantity _____ × $16.95 per book: AMOUNT: _____

FL Res. Sales Tax (COUNTY: _____):   TAX: _____

Priority Shipping ($4.50, 50¢ each add'l book):   SHIPPING: _____

       TOTAL: _____

Ship To (*for gifts, see next page*)

NAME: _____

ADDRESS: _____

CITY, STATE, ZIP: _____

DAYTIME PHONE: (_____) _____

☐ This is a gift (*see next page*).
☐ Please add my name to your mailing list. Let me know about
   speaking engagements, workshops, new books and tapes.
☐ Send announcements to my email: _____

Ordering as a Gift

QUANTITY: _____

GIFT FOR: _____

ADDRESS: _____

CITY, STATE, ZIP: _____

MESSAGE: _____

_____

_____

_____

QUANTITY: _____

GIFT FOR: _____

ADDRESS: _____

CITY, STATE, ZIP: _____

MESSAGE: _____

_____

_____

_____

QUANTITY: _____

GIFT FOR: _____

ADDRESS: _____

CITY, STATE, ZIP: _____

MESSAGE: _____

_____

_____